JOHN NEWTON

Author of *Amazing Grace*

Anne Sandberg

BARBOUR
PUBLISHING, INC.
Uhrichsville, Ohio

Other books in the "Heroes of the Faith" series:

Brother Andrew
Gladys Aylward
William and Catherine Booth
John Bunyan
William Carey
Amy Carmichael
George Washington Carver
Fanny Crosby
Frederick Douglass
Jonathan Edwards
Jim Elliot
Charles Finney
Billy Graham
C. S. Lewis
Eric Liddell
David Livingstone
Martin Luther
D. L. Moody

Samuel Morris
George Müller
Watchman Nee
Florence Nightingale
Luis Palau
Francis and Edith Schaeffer
Charles Sheldon
Mary Slessor
Charles Spurgeon
John and Betty Stam
Hudson Taylor
William Tyndale
Corrie ten Boom
Mother Teresa
Sojourner Truth
John Wesley
George Whitefield

Published by Barbour Publishing, Inc., P.O. Box 719, Uhrichsville, OH 44683 http://www.barbourbooks.com

Cover illustration © Dick Bobnick.

Member of the
Evangelical Christian
Publishers Association

Printed in the United States of America.

JOHN NEWTON

preface

For over 200 years the song "Amazing Grace" by John Newton has been loved and sung by Christians worldwide. It is included in the hymnals of most traditional and evangelical churches. Almost everyone knows the first verse by memory:

> *Amazing grace, how sweet the sound,*
> *That saved a wretch like me.*
> *I once was lost but now am found,*
> *Was blind, but now I see.*

But not everyone knows that when Newton wrote that song he was not being merely poetic, but truthful and grateful. Few who sing those words know how much of a wretch he really had been—how sinful, how blasphemous, how licentious and rebellious against God and man.

Nor do many know of his great love for a woman which sustained him through his terrible punishment as a deserter from the British navy; through his humiliations while engaged in the slave trade; through being shipwrecked. These were some of the "many dangers, toils and snares" through which he had "already come."

Eventually this sinful atheist became a famous minister, writer, and hymnwriter.

In the early days of his walk with God, he was influenced by the great Wesleyan and Whitefield revivals. Also, because of his experiences in the slave trade, he was one of the early supporters of the abolition of slavery in England.

Since Newton lived over 200 years ago I have had to imagine details of his actions, thoughts and events. However, the "imaginative" part is not merely fanciful but an attempt to visualize just how and what happened, keeping true to facts known and recorded, which included real names of people, places and ships.

The factual material in this book was obtained from the biography of John Newton written by Bernard Martin of England (now out of print). Mr. Martin had access to Newton's letters, diaries, slave-trading journal, etc. I have used this biography as source for the facts, dates, names of people, places and ships. I consider this book to be completely authentic.

I have also used material from *An Authentic Narrative*, an autobiography by Newton himself, written in 1764. Since this volume is quite brief and incomplete, I believe my account of his life will give a fuller knowledge and appreciation of this man who, because of God's amazing grace to him, became a well-known man of God in his day.

Anne Sandberg

one

*The Story of John Newton
Who Wrote "Amazing Grace"*

ARLY ON a December morning in 1742, young John Newton began his long hike out of London—his lean, sea-bronzed face betraying lack of enthusiasm. "Always have to do what the old gentleman says," he grumbled. "I'll be glad when I'm back at sea, away from his nagging."

Morosely, he strode through the narrow cobblestone streets, head down, mind churning with rebellion against his father. At the outskirts of the city, he found the stables and rented a horse for the trip which, unknown to him, was to shape the rest of his life.

"How far to Maidstone?" he asked the proprietor, digging into his pocket for the money.

"If you take the shortcut through the woods, it will be about fifty kilometers." The man eyed the blue-checked middy blouse, long, wide trousers and flat cap of the youth. "What's a sailor doing on a horse?" he quipped. "Out to see one of your lady friends before sailing?"

Annoyed by the obvious reference to "A girl in every port," and offended by his impertinence, Newton replied coldly, "Nothing like that. Just an errand for my father."

He paid the fee and leaped onto the horse. The proprietor, hands on hips, watched him disappear in a spray of snow. "These young fellows! Nothing but speed, speed. He'll kill that old mare."

John didn't think it necessary to satisfy the curiosity of the man by informing him that after he had finished his father's business in Maidstone, he was going a few miles north, to the Catlett home in Chatham.

As he bolted through the woods he thought wryly, *It would be more exciting if I were going to spend the evening with a luscious young wench instead of an old woman I hardly know.*

He slowed his pace while he wrapped his woolen scarf once more around his throat, shivering in the cold and mumbling discontentedly.

"What an idiot I am! Father sends me on an errand to Maidstone and what do I do but tell him, 'Mrs. Catlett wrote that if I am ever in her vicinity, to stop by....'

"And what does the old gentleman do—instead of just giving his consent, he practically orders: 'After you finish the business at Maidstone—before you return to London—I want you to visit Mrs. Catlett. It's close by.'"

John's face registered a strange blend of distaste and rebellion.

Urging his horse faster, he plunged through the unfamiliar terrain, with regard neither for his old steed nor for himself. Twice the horse tripped over snow-covered stumps, the second time Newton's hat fell off. Cursing, he stopped to retrieve it, shook off the snow and characteristically blamed the nearest object—the horse. "Drat this old mare! That fellow must have rented me the worst nag in the stables. Just like the rest of the old folks; can't trust a young fellow!"

He stopped at Maidstone and tended to his father's business. Then he leaped back onto his horse and began on a gallop toward Chatham. Suddenly he stopped. "I don't know about going there," he mused. "I'm not doing it! She invited me, but I didn't make any promises...." As he sat on the horse, irresolute, the beast began to tremble with the cold, so with a shrug, John said, "All right, let's go."

His brow puckered as he galloped along. "What will I do at the Catlett's place?" (Even his experience as a rookie sailor had not cured him of his basic shyness and dread of meeting new people.) "What will I say? I don't have polished manners. Been with roughs too much. All I'm used to is sailor talk, plus liquor, curses; women, curses, drunken brawls, curses...What if I accidentally let loose a curse word? What if...

"Well, how *do* you behave in genteel society?

"'Pleased to meet you, Mrs. Catlett. How are you? And how are the children?'" (He heard there were five.)

"Drat it, that's no way to talk to a person who was so kind to my sick mother. I'm *obligated* to her...Oh, how I hate being obligated to anybody...But I am...I should be...

"Maybe I should say, 'Mrs. Catlett, I appreciate so

much what you did for my mother during her last illness....' No, I might break down. What would they think of a seventeen-year-old boy, man, sailor, whatever ...shedding tears?"

For ten miles he worried as he galloped through woods, past snow-covered fields, past farm houses nestled snuggly in small plots of land—all looking so tranquil in contrast to his inward turmoil.

Suddenly, he slowed his pace. He had been thinking so hard that he had not been paying attention to his surroundings. "Where on earth am I by now?" he exclaimed. As he looked around, he noticed the cottages huddled more and more closely.

"Oh, no, I'll soon be there! I've got to think up the right thing to say." He frowned deeply then quickly brightened. "Why not just be myself! That's right. Just say what's natural, and that would be—of course—the first thing I'd want to do is express my appreciation for Mrs. Catlett's care of Mother."

His mother.

It had been ten years ago when he was only seven. For a long time his mother had been ailing; and then, that awful day! He would always remember it. (His father, Captain Newton, was at sea and would not return for about a year.) Then she came—that kind Mrs. Catlett— and said, "Johnny, your mother is very sick and must get away from London. It is bad for consumption. I'm going to take her to my country home in Chatham and nurse her."

His eyes alight with excitement, he had eagerly turned

to his mother. "When are we going, Mama?"

"I am sorry, my son," his mother had replied (fixing those big, sunken eyes on his face, so tenderly, so sadly); "but you must stay here with neighbors until your father returns from the sea."

How could he ever forget that terrible, that heart-breaking moment! "No, Mama, no. Don't leave me. Please, Mama." Sobbing, he had flung himself into her arms.

Holding him tightly, stroking his head, his mother had told him, "Now be a little man. Don't cry anymore. After I get well, I will come back to you. I will pray for you every day. God will take care of you."

It wasn't only the anguish of being parted from his mother that terrified the child, but the prospect of being now in the care of his austere, seafaring father whom he seldom saw and whom he feared.

For a long moment mother and son had clung together, then Mrs. Newton pulled herself away. Through tear-blurred eyes Johnny had watched Mrs. Catlett support his mother (so weak that she could hardly step up into the carriage). Still sobbing, little John had gazed as the carriage got smaller and smaller and then was out of sight. He never saw his mother again. It had been a fatal illness. And now ten years later, John had received a letter from Mrs. Catlett saying, "If you are ever in this vicinity, why not visit us?"

(Previously John's father had prevailed upon a wealthy merchant friend, Joseph Manesty, to get John a job in Jamaica. But since it would be two weeks before sailing time, his father had sent John on this errand.)

Now John's gallop became a trot, then a slow walk as he looked around. Stopping at the nearest cottage, he inquired as to where the Catletts lived. A middle-aged woman, vigorously shoveling her walk, paused in her task long enough to give directions.

The house was easy to find—a rather large, two-story dwelling surrounded by a white fence, a spacious yard on each side and trees in the back. Slowly dismounting, John braced himself. The dreaded moment had come.

two

The Catlett Home

TYING HIS horse to a post, John pushed open the gate then stood stock still as a dog bounded toward him barking furiously; chickens squawked and the cat fled in alarm. Not anxious to have an encounter with the dog, John dared not proceed. In a moment the front door opened and people poured out: a stocky, hardy-looking man, a plump, pink-cheeked woman of middle age, a youth, three young children, and a pretty girl, maybe sixteen.

Before he could begin his rehearsed speech, Mrs. Catlett threw her arms around him. "Of course you are John. You look just like your dear mother, God bless her memory."

The rest of the family crowded around. First, Mr. Catlett placed his hand on John's shoulder in a friendly gesture. Next, the youth shook his hand, the children stared and the girl smiled shyly—no, not exactly shyly; she was friendly and winsome. (Not brazen like the girls he had met at seaports. No, not like them. This girl was different.)

"Come in, come in," cried Mrs. Catlett, leading the way. "Do sit down, you must be tired. Jack, take his horse to the barn." John walked into the living room and sat stiffly in the comfortable chair she offered near the fireplace. The others stood or sat nearby. For a while John held his hat on his lap, feeling rather nervous, until the young girl Mary smilingly took it from him and hung it in the hall.

John quickly surveyed the room. It was large and many-windowed. The furniture was more durable than elegant, yet homey and comfortable looking, bearing the marks of years of wear.

And now began the happy confusion of questions and comments. "How far did you travel? How long can you stay? It's hard to realize that that little boy of seven is now such a handsome young man."

After the chatter subsided, Mrs. Catlett and Mary bustled into the kitchen for refreshments. Their departure left an awkward silence. No one seemed to have anything more to say. The ticking of the clock accentuated the silence. Then the cat came to the rescue. He leaped onto John's lap and began purring.

"I hope you don't mind the cat," apologized Mr. Catlett. His quiet voice belied the rugged strength of his appearance, his large, rough hands, his broad, muscled shoulders. Instinctively, John knew that this man was not adept at making conversation.

"No, I don't mind," said John as he stroked the cat. "I never had a pet when I was a child, so I enjoy this little creature."

"I'm glad you feel that way," Mr. Catlett replied. The silence which followed confirmed John's feeling that neither Mr. Catlett nor his son Jack were very communicative. But to John's relief, the children began telling of the escapades of their cat and dog—"Once our dog..." And so the time passed pleasantly.

John was relieved to see the two ladies emerge from the kitchen with tea and little cakes.

Whether deliberately or accidentally, Mary sat directly across from him in full view of his appreciative glances. Mr. Catlett and Jack took opposite sides of the table and the children sat in between. For the next few minutes, everyone was occupied with eating (mother signaling to the small children lest they should take more than a discreet portion). In between mouthfuls, they all plied John with more questions.

John tried to answer them all. To Mrs. Catlett he said, "My father is in the West Indies getting slaves. He'll sell most of them to the American colonies—they use them on their big plantations."

Jack, the youth his own age, questioned, "What do you think of the slave trade?"

John turned toward the young man, looking into alert and intelligent eyes.

"I haven't given much thought to it. It's a very profitable business and beneficial to the savages. Whoever buys them will teach them civil manners and of course, religion."

"Yes," replied Jack, his manner indicating a readiness

to argue, "but do you think it is right to sell people like cattle?"

Looking embarrassed, Jack's father interrupted, "My son is attending law school and has acquired some liberal ideas. Don't take him too seriously."

(But Jack's question sank into the deep recesses of John's mind, to bear fruit years later.)

And the girl, smiling at him across the table, asked, "How do you like being a sailor? To get to see different lands?" John liked the way she tilted her head, dreamily looking off into the distance, then turning to him for his reply.

He looked at her so often that he was afraid it would be noticed. *Charming*, he found himself thinking. *Could she read his thoughts? Did she see his interest?* He stumbled a little as he answered her questions, angry at himself when he blushed.

Unaware of John's embarrassment at the betrayal of his interest in her daughter, Mrs. Catlett kept on talking. "Do you remember much about your mother? You were not quite seven when she—went to her eternal reward."

Before he could answer she turned to the children. "Now you must leave some of those cakes for our special guest." Then she settled more comfortably into her chair and looked at John. He had already framed his answer to her first question, when he discovered she had a disconcerting way of losing the trend and changing to other subjects.

"Your mother declared she was surely going to heaven.

You know, the Church of England discourages such claims of familiarity with God. It's best to leave those matters with the parson." She paused a moment and seemed to peer at John for his answer. It made him feel uncomfortable. But she unabashedly continued, "Of course, you know your mother was a Dissenter. Or perhaps you were too young to understand."

Mr. Catlett and Jack exchanged glances. Mother was talkative—there was no way of stopping her. But why did she get on this controversial subject?

Looking a little puzzled, John replied, "I do remember a little about that. Father was a moral man but had no religious leanings. Still, he didn't object to mother's associations with the Dissenters. She took me to their meetings. Mother was very pious and taught me a lot of...religion...and other things."

"Indeed she taught you many things," exclaimed Mrs. Catlett. "She told me you could read scripture at age four. And Latin at age six."

She looked into the faces of her younger children, who seemed more interested in cookies than in Latin. "See," their mother said, "if you apply yourselves like John did, you can learn too." Then she signaled Mary to move the cookies less temptingly near the children.

Looking amused at the gesture, John turned to his hostess: "I guess I was different from most children. I would rather stay indoors and study with Mother than go out to play." He saw the children's faces cloud with dismay at the price to pay for learning Latin by age six. "Of course," he added hastily, "it's fine for children to play; it makes them strong in body and happy in spirit." The children sighed with relief.

"She gave me lessons out of Isaac Watts' book for children, *Preservatives from the Sins and Follies of Youth.* I memorized the whole book."

"Oh we have that book," one of the children broke in. "But Mama doesn't ask us to memorize it; she just reads it to us and asks questions."

Another child jumped up saying, "I'll get it," pushed his chair from the table and headed for the bookcase. Upon that Mrs. Catlett remarked, "Perhaps we should all go into the parlor; the chairs are more comfortable. And John, you take the same chair beside the fireplace."

"Here's the book," the child said, handing it to John. "Oh thank you," John said, his face alight with memories as he turned the pages.

three

Stories in the Parlor

A s THE various family members settled in chairs near him, John inwardly groaned at the thought of the "sins and follies of youth" which he had already committed. And of his present doubts as to the existence of God; for another book was influencing him at this time—the one written by atheist Lord Shaftesbury.

Mrs. Catlett leaned toward John, "Your mother said you read and memorized scripture and sang hymns together. Do you remember any of them?"

"Oh Mrs. Catlett," demurred John, "I am a lover of music but please don't ask me to sing!" And the family laughed. How charming Mary looked, her cheeks flushed with laughter, a wisp of hair across her cheek.

For a moment they listened to the mantle clock chime the hour, then Mrs. Catlett had another question. "I often wondered what happened when your father came back and learned that your mother had died. I mean, here is a sea captain, so often away on long trips and with a child to be responsible for."

Looking down, John hesitated. He didn't want to talk about this painful time. *How can I get out of this?* he thought. *Without offending Mrs. Catlett.* But when he saw the look of interest in Mary's eyes he decided to talk.

"My father remarried and we moved to Avon. Afterwards they sent me to a boarding school in Essex. My first schoolmaster was very cruel. I wasn't a model child...I did get into mischief. But that man beat me for trifles and often sent me to bed without meals. I hated him."

Mary looked distressed. "But why did you let him; why didn't you...I guess you couldn't run away...Oh, I'm so sorry."

Mrs. Catlett patted his arm. "You poor dear." And in the eyes of the rest of the family, he saw genuine sympathy.

What a time John was having! Never in all his life (except the first seven years when he was his mother's darling) had he experienced anything like this. At his present home he was just a step-somebody, the son of a stern father who was often away. And on board the ships he was just a crew member. But these people really seemed to care!

And John reveled in the aura and warmth of this new and reassuring experience. It took him off guard and encouraged him to say more in one afternoon than he had to any other person since his mother's death. The closed door of his heart began to swing open and the buried events of his miserable later childhood flowed out into the sunlight of this loving family.

It was time, John realized. For with his naturally retiring personality, he was becoming more and more withdrawn, more of a misanthrope, not caring for anyone, almost hating some. It was his reaction to a world he felt was unsympathetic to him. If his father and stepmother didn't care for him, why should he care for them; in fact, why should he care for anybody? He would be for himself and to himself...But now, something new was happening, at least for the moment. And his reserve melted in the warmth of this atmosphere.

He continued his story. "After those first two years under that cruel schoolmaster things finally did improve. My heartache over losing Mother eased, and I got a better schoolmaster."

As though listening to a bard, the family members leaned forward eagerly.

"Well, John," said Mrs. Catlett, "your mother prayed so much for you when she was with us, that I am sure the good Lord watched over you."

At this remark John assumed that the family must be very religious so he thought they would be pleased to hear of some of the providences of God in his life.

"Yes, a number of times I was kept from either death or at least serious accident." For some reason John glanced in the direction of Jack and saw something in his attitude which made him hesitate a moment. Was Jack skeptical about religious matters? Did his studies in law school turn him away from God? But why was he, John, disturbed by that? Didn't he have his own doubts about God?

Acutely sensitive to the negative reactions of those around him, John almost decided not to tell the story, lest he should earn Jack's scorn. But when he saw the interest of the children, he decided to proceed, directing the story to them.

"After a while my stepmother had three children and I guess she got too busy to pay much attention to me. My father was away at sea so often. I was very lonely and so found friends in the street. But they taught me to swear and do other bad things.

"Anyway, one day when I was eleven I was riding a horse when he tripped and threw me over his head toward a newly cut hedge. I just missed being pierced by thick, sharp stakes. I could have been killed or badly hurt. I got up from my fall and said to myself, 'God is punishing me for being so bad.' But as I thought more about it, I said to myself, 'Maybe God is showing me His goodness by not letting me get hurt.' I wasn't sure which. Anyway, I stopped swearing and was a good boy." (John didn't say, however, that his reform was very brief.)

Sighing with relief at the happy ending, the children asked, "Have you any more stories about when you were a child?"

"Not exactly a child, I was about fifteen, a little younger than your sister Mary.

"Oh," said the boy, "Mary's only fourteen, but she looks older."

"Well, whatever," John said, smiling warmly at Mary.

"Some of us boys planned to go to the Thames River to see a Man-O-War at anchor, so we set the time when we would meet at the wharf the next day. My stepmother had an errand for me, so I was delayed. When I arrived a little late, I saw the boys were already in the small boat rowing towards the ship. One of them was my best friend."

John paused a moment as he remembered. (Of course, he didn't tell how angry he had been, and how he shook his fist and cursed the boys for going without him.)

"What happened then?" the children cried.

"It was very sad. The sea was rough and as I stood on shore watching their boat bob up and down, a big wave overturned the boat. It was awful seeing them thrashing around in the waves. They all drowned. It was a terrible experience. But as I thought it over, I realized it was the hand of Providence that I was not in that boat, or I too would have drowned."

"Of course it was," broke in Mrs. Catlett. "I know God answered your mother's prayer. She had always prayed that you would become a parson."

John stared at her. "A parson! Did she tell you that? Well, I...I guess Mother meant well. She was very religious."

During the conversation, John's eyes frequently wandered across the room toward Mary. Once their eyes met, and she turned away, blushing. (The girls at the sea ports didn't blush. Mary was so sweet, so pure, so lovely. He determined that during his visit, he would spend time with her.)

As the children begged for more stories, the mantle clock bonged. They had spent a good part of the afternoon with John. Mrs. Catlett jumped up. "Oh goodness me, it's five o'clock, and I must get dinner. Mary, light the candles and then come into the kitchen. John must be starved after his long journey.

"John, you talk with Mr. Catlett. Jack has to study for an examination. And you children go to your rooms and don't bother John any more asking for stories. He can tell you more later." She turned to John, "You'll stay a while, won't you?"

"Yes, Mrs. Catlett, I'd love to," he replied, forgetting his earlier resolve to get away as soon as possible.

As he watched Mary light the candles, he thought, *How graceful, how lovely she is*. And then with a smile, she left and went into the kitchen.

The two men sat before the fireplace watching the flames, saying nothing. It was apparent that both were uncomfortable.

four

John and Mr. Catlett

*T*HEN THE dog arose from his slumber, yawned and walked to John, asking for attention. Smiling, he stood up and rubbed the animal under its chin. "Quite a friendly fellow," remarked Mr. Catlett. "He would probably wag his tail at a burglar and ask for a head rub."

Both men laughed. Then silence.

When John took his seat again and looked at Mr. Catlett he saw in his host's face something which he had surmised all the time the family had been conversing at the table, Mrs. Catlett doing most of the talking.

Mr. Catlett was shy and was feeling ill at ease at being alone with him and having to entertain him! Here was a kindred spirit, one which John understood very well— this inward torment at being unable to communicate and share himself with others.

Although he had opened his heart so freely to the family, now in the presence of this equally reserved man, John again felt tongue-tied and tense. So now each would be trying, perhaps straining to prevent awkward silences.

John could sense that Mr. Catlett was trying valiantly to be the genial host. "How are things in your home, John, with your new mother and everything?"

In an effort to communicate, John replied, "I was only ten when my father remarried. I don't know, it seemed to me that I was sort of—in the way—like I was coming between her and my father. I don't believe she ever cared for me.

"And I know that my father never did, never, even when my own mother was living. He was away on trips so often, and when he would come home, he was like a stranger. That's why I clung so to my mother. She was all I had."

John paused, waiting for a comment from Mr. Catlett, but receiving none, he continued. "My father was so cold and aloof, I was really afraid of him when I was little. And as I got older, all I got from him was correction, correction. Sometimes I almost hated him."

John was so aroused by the release of his pent-up feelings that he arose and stood in front of the fireplace. Mr. Catlett stood beside him and laid his hand on John's arm. "John, I have five children and know how often it is necessary to correct them. Don't you think that you may have been perhaps a little overly sensitive? It is hard for me to believe that your father didn't love you."

John struggled to control his emotions, surprised at the bitterness emerging from within. "Then why didn't he show it? At least once in his life. But he never did. Never.

"When I was eleven, he began taking me on trips to teach me the trade. We occupied the captain's cabin, slept together, ate together and even then he remained distant."

"Perhaps, John, he wasn't cold; perhaps he felt deeply about you but was unable to express it. Some people are like that. It may be that he wished you would show him affection also."

John looked at Mr. Catlett, startled at the suggestion, then mumbled, "Perhaps, perhaps."

Mr. Catlett continued in his gentle way. "I can understand a personality like that." He looked a little wistful. "Fortunately, I have a wife and daughter who are very outgoing."

Smiling, John replied, "Yes, I can see that."

Again the two were silent, each engaged with his own thoughts, when one of the children burst into the room. "Mama says everything is ready. We have roast and peas and pudding; she even got out some of the cake she was saving for Christmas. Oh boy, John, am I ever glad you came!"

Smiling broadly, the two men arose and went into the dining room. During the meal, John suddenly felt drained and tired. He had opened his heart to this family much more than he had realized. In fact, it was the first time he had really expressed some of his deeply buried feelings. But now he felt the old shyness tighten up his heart and lips, and he said very little.

After the meal, while the women were in the kitchen,

Jack returned to his studying and the children to playing. In the front room with Mr. Catlett, John looked over to a bookshelf and his eyes lighted up. "I see you have some interesting books."

"Do you like to read?"

"Oh yes, I'm a great reader. I see you have Benet's *Christian Oratory* and *Family Instruction.* I've read them and well—look here." Surprised, he picked up *Characteristics* by Lord Shaftesbury. "How did this book get here?"

Looking embarrassed, Mr. Catlett tried to explain. I know that Lord Shaftesbury is an atheist. I didn't want that book in the house. But Jack thinks we should be enlightened and read other's viewpoints...I really..."

"Well, well," replied John thoughtfully; "if you don't mind, I'd like to look this book over."

"Why certainly, just go ahead. I have some chores outside; do you mind being alone for a while?"

"Not at all," replied John and after Mr. Catlett left, he sank into his comfortable chair and opened the book. But he couldn't read; he just held the book, engulfed in gloomy thoughts. He sank deeper into his chair, looking out of the window at the snow-covered garden.

When he was joined an hour later by Mrs. Catlett and Mary, he was embarrassed to discover that he had been dozing. Was that amusement in Mary's eyes? How humiliating! He would have to make up some reason, some excuse, but Mrs. Catlett came to his rescue.

"You poor dear; you've had a long and wearisome

day. What with that long journey on horseback and all of our questioning, you must be very tired."

John sat up straight, put on his most alert expression (while throwing sidelong glances at Mary). "Oh, no, Mrs. Catlett, I guess it was the soothing effect of the fire-place."

In a moment members of the family reappeared from wherever they had been. The children eagerly crowded around John. "Tell us more stories about when you were a boy," they cried, sitting down before him.

In alarm, John looked from their eager faces into the face of Mr. Catlett, then his wife.

"Not tonight, children," said Mr. Catlett. "John will be here for awhile, and you will have plenty of stories later." In his heart John was hoping that rather than spending time telling children stories, that he could be with Mary.

For another hour the evening wore on slowly, until it was obvious that it was time to retire.

five

Thinking in the Night

T HAT NIGHT as John lay on a soft feather bed (instead of a ship's hammock), his mind was such a tangle of thoughts that he couldn't fall asleep. *Mary. Mary. Is this "love at first sight"? That's foolish; I always scoffed at the notion. But is this what happened to me today? Why do I feel so deeply about her, having known her for just a few hours? How does she feel about me? Of course, she isn't even thinking about me.*

Then her parents, what kind of impression did I make? What chance do I have with this family, so refined, so superior to me. I'm unpolished and overly serious. I'm not a socializer.

Still, I was surprised, totally surprised at how much this family drew out of me tonight! Maybe I'm not a complete introvert; maybe I have potential. I never thought so before.

Then there's the matter of making a living; I don't have a steady job, can't ever seem to keep one. No, I'm not much of a prospect for Mary. I'll just have to forget all about it. Besides she's only fourteen, and I'm seventeen. It's just a hopeless dream.

He sighed, turned over on his side and tried to sleep. But he was too wide awake; too many thoughts flooded his mind. He turned again and lay on his back, hands under his head and just let the thoughts flow—no use even trying to sleep.

This book I found on their book shelf, the one by Lord Shaftesbury—what is it doing in this home? They seem to go to church. What would they think if they knew about my lack of religion? What would Mary think?

Then in an effort to justify himself, he thought about that period in his life between his fifteenth and seventeenth years. He had become so disturbed by his sinfulness that he decided to seek God—fasting, praying, reading scripture and pious books. He even refrained from meat for three months as a penance and avoided people so much that he became gloomy and unsociable.

And it worked for a while. But after reading the books by Lord Shaftesbury something began to happen to him. He didn't realize it then, but it was like a slow poison, until gradually he became an atheist himself.

It was still vivid in his mind when the change began. He had come ashore from a trip with his father. As he had strolled through the narrow cobblestone streets of the Dutch seaport of Middleburg, looking into the windows of the various small shops, as usual he had sought out the bookshop.

In the window he was surprised to find among all the Dutch titles one book with an English title: *Characteristics*. He entered the shop and picked up the volume. *A forbidden book,* he had thought, *dangerous*. Its author was Lord Shaftesbury, a known freethinker and atheist. After a momentary feeling of guilt and impulse to put down the book, he had rationalized, *This is just what a young man needs to have his mind expanded, to be informed of another viewpoint.*

And he walked out of the store, book under arm, not realizing that he had reached a turning point in his life which was drastically to alter his lifestyle for years and nearly cost him his soul. Later he bought *Rhapsody*, by the same author.

After that, on future trips with his father he had become so immersed in this newest book that he hardly paid attention to the instructions in seamanship his father attempted to give him. *Well,* he had thought, *who said I wanted to be a sailor anyway; it was my father's idea to follow in his steps.* John tensed in bed as he remembered the day his father had stormed, "I wish you would put away your books. You're supposed to be a sailor, but your mind is always in the clouds. You'll never be anything but an impractical dreamer, never amount to anything!"

Dreamer, John had thought, *why I'm a philosopher, a thinker, that's what I'm cut out to be.* Of course, he wouldn't have said that to his father; for he was sure the captain would have called it plain indolence or in plainer language, laziness.

Characteristically, John had lifted his chin, pursed his lips but didn't dare say what he wanted to—that his father was an old fogey who didn't believe in progress; that everyone with intelligence was reading Shaftesbury. And if religion couldn't be questioned, what was it worth?

Actually, his own brand of religion hadn't amounted to much. He always loved the ways of the world, enjoyed his sins. But there remained in him enough of his mother's teachings to make him fear hell. So at times he grudgingly read pious books and said a few prayers— just enough to salve his conscience. And then he would feel free to go out for a night of sin.

With that kind of insincerity, he was an easy prey for Shaftesbury's arguments that there was no hell or heaven, nor God nor devils nor angels.

Having that background his associations with the sailors precipitated his slide downward. He began to curse and even blaspheme and mock anything that pertained to God and religion and the Bible.

(Strange, that his interest in Mary should awaken a conscience which had long ago ceased to trouble him!)

Finishing his introspection, the youth thought, *So this is the kind of person I am. What can I offer Mary? The Catletts have no idea what I'm really like. What if they should discover my unbelief; my licentiousness, my foul mouth? What if they should learn about my rebellion against discipline, my irresponsibility?*

At least, he thought defensively, *that's what my father says about me!*

He tossed and turned in bed, listened to the sounds of the countryside, the barking of the dog, the neighing of his horse, the creak of the tree outside his window. Finally, as it began to dawn, he heard the faint crow of a rooster, and he fell asleep.

The smell of bacon and hot griddle cakes wafting up into his bedroom awakened him pleasantly. For a while he lazily breathed in the fragrance, then realized with a start that he must be sleeping late (as usual). He bounded out of bed, dressed quickly and hurried downstairs into the kitchen.

At breakfast he found Mary more charming and vivacious than ever. "We're going to a social event this afternoon, John," she said with a saucy smile. "Mother said she would love to have the sailor boy come along."

"Count me in, Mary," he replied, trying not to betray his too great delight. On the way he managed to walk with Mary, stifling his desire to catch hold of her hand. But she seemed archly unaware of his interest. "How long before you have to leave?" she asked.

"No special time; my ship won't be sailing for a while. I'll stay as long as your family can put up with me." He tried to sound casual. Now was not the time to tell her that his ship was to sail from Liverpool for Jamaica in less than two weeks.

His father had asked and received a favor from Joseph Manesty, a wealthy merchant in the shipping business. Young Englishmen were needed to manage large sugar plantations in Jamaica. Besides a good salary, there were opportunities to earn extra money, so it was a wonderful prospect for the future. Within five years he could acquire a goodly sum and return to England with a comfortable income. Naturally, his father had been pleased with this future for his son.

But now that John was in love, he would never let such mundane matters as the pursuit of money interfere with his pursuit of a dream.

The days passed swiftly. He fell so completely in love with Mary that it was obvious to the family, and they began to tease him about her. But he knew that even though Mary apparently enjoyed his company, she by no means shared his ardor. She was really too young, yet seemed so mature in actions and appearance. After all, girls in those days often married at fifteen. Of course, John wasn't thinking of marriage yet, but he knew he had found *the girl*.

Carefully John marked the time, counting the days. Yes, the ship had sailed by now, without him. That was the way he wanted it, the way he planned it. After all, this trip would have taken five years and by the time he would have returned, Mary would be nineteen and surely married by then. No, that must never be. He couldn't bear to think of losing her to someone else.

Finally, the day came when he knew he couldn't stay any longer. He and Mary and Mrs. Catlett walked to the barn where his horse had been kept. Not daring to express his feelings in the presence of her mother, John looked into Mary's face one last time, his eyes alight with love.

He held her hand as long as he dared, then mounted his horse. With one long lingering look, he galloped away.

For miles his thoughts were occupied with Mary. But as he neared London, he began to worry. *I've done it again; lost another job. Now I've got to face the old gentleman, and he'll be furious. What excuse can I frame up this time?*

six

The Trip Back to London

JOHN HAD been travelling a short time when it began to snow. "Drat it!" he groaned. "Now this, on top of my misery! Oh my aching heart, to have to part from my beloved!" For the next few miles, he engaged in massive self-pity, considering himself to be the most wretched young man in England.

But the closer he got to London (and his father) the less he thought of his heartache, and the more he gave way to the dread of facing the Captain's wrath.

"But why should I fear him?" he countered rebelliously. "What does he care about me? What has he ever done for me? Well, a few things...but not that much...mostly giving me lectures." He began to feel good as he attempted to justify his many misdemeanors.

The more his thoughts churned in his mind, the more he comforted himself that *he* was the one being mistreated. He felt so sorry for himself that his eyes overflowed with tears, to mingle with the melting snow on his face.

Meanwhile the storm increased until he stopped under a broad tree and huddled miserably over his panting horse. *Might be a good thing if I got sick and came home coughing and wheezing, then maybe he wouldn't be so hard on me.* With that "happy" thought, he resumed his journey through the snow-clogged woods and finally came out into a clearing. On the highway he went into a full gallop, his wet clothing flopping against his chilled body.

As the miles sped by, his mind was busily engaged, going from subject to subject, scene to scene; sometimes it was Mary, then his father, then Mr. Catlett.

Finally, he saw in the distance more familiar terrain and realized there were just a few more kilometers before he reached his destination. How he dreaded that meeting!

He knew what his father would say—throw up to him that episode in Alicante—he was always doing that. What an experience that had been! His shoulders tightened as he remembered that time.

One day his father had said, "John, I am planning to retire, but before I do, I want to settle you in some kind of work. You're fifteen and old enough to think seriously of your lifetime profession." John pressed his lips together as he remembered his own unspoken reactions at that time: "Try and make me," but it was useless to buck his father, and in the end he had to comply.

So he had been apprenticed to work in the office of a Spanish businessman in Alicante, Spain. True, John liked mathematics and was good at figures. He learned the trade quickly, but all the while he thought, *This old bird has such outdated methods, I'll use my own. They're much more efficient.*

But his master was horrified. "No, you don't do it that way, but this way; understand, my way, not yours."

"But can't you see that your way takes much longer," John had argued.

"Never mind 'much longer'; you do as I say," his master had insisted.

But John had rebelliously gone ahead with his own faster methods. So what happens? His father comes scuttling over on the next ship, asking, "What's the problem, boy? Why can't you get along?"

And John spouted, "I'm not going to let this foreigner tell me what to do and how to do it. I know a few things myself!"

"But that's what is expected when you are apprenticed."

"All the same, I don't like it," John had sputtered.

The result was that John had been discharged for "unsettled behavior and impatience of restraint." He winced now as he remembered how angry and disappointed his father had been. Now, not only was his father obliged to postpone his retirement, but also had to find another job for his son.

After that episode, his father had taken him on several of his own voyages. They shared the same cabin and yet he and his father seemed miles apart. *Some father,* John had thought bitterly. *He jokes and laughs with his second mate and even with some of the sailors. But not with me. Yeah, some father!* Angrily, he swished the snow off his face. *Curses on this storm! When will it stop?*

For a while he galloped along—almost spent with anger at his father, at the weather, at the world. Then his thoughts brought him back to the very recent past, in fact, just a few weeks ago. His father had finally decided to go ahead with his retirement plans and bluntly said to John:

"I'm going to get you a job where you will have to work, and where you won't be able to waste your time dreaming and reading books. You're going to have to support yourself."

With rebellion in his heart, John had listened, but as usual, feared and respected his father enough not to dare express his feelings.

"John," his father had continued, "I'm beginning to think you are not cut out to be a sailor. So I have asked my friend Joseph Manesty to give you a job, and he said he has just the thing for you. They're wanting young Englishmen in Jamaica to manage their sugar plantations. You will have good food, good pay and a promising future. The ship will be sailing from Liverpool in two weeks."

"How long will I be gone?" John had asked.

"About five years."

"Five years!" John had stormed. "That's a long, long time." Finally however, he had reluctantly agreed.

As John thought of the day he was to leave home for

the long sea journey, he again felt a surge of self-pity. How gleefully his stepmother had packed his sea chest! Bitterly, he had thought, *She's glad to get rid of me.* Then had come the time to say goodby and of course his father could not refrain from lecturing him: "Now you make good this time. Don't make a mess of it like you did in Spain, you hear?" (Wonderful farewell words to remember of his loving father!)

John was to meet Mr. Manesty in Liverpool, but since the coach would not be leaving from London for a while, his father had sent him on an errand to Maidstone, suggesting at the time that John accept the invitation to visit the Catlett home in nearby Chatham.

But now he had concluded his visit to Chatham, had taken his last lingering look at Mary, and had finally left, deliberately overstaying his time. And here he was, heading for home, two weeks past sailing time, about to encounter the wrath of his father. And of course, the disdain of his stepmother. (So she wasn't getting rid of him after all!)

As the spires of London came into view, John abruptly stopped his musings, braced himself and spurred on his horse for the last stretch. Miles before, he had already planned an excuse: "I didn't realize the time was past. Mrs. Catlett had been so kind to Mother, I felt obligated to stay a while. I didn't...I couldn't..." Oh what was the use! He knew his lies would have no weight whatsoever with his father. So he gave up any further thinking of what he would say.

When he reached the stables where he had rented his horse, he flung himself off, squared his shoulders and began slogging over the slushy snow toward his home.

seven

Other Voyages
"The Press Gang"

IS FEET dragging as he turned into his own street, John attempted in vain to force a few coughs. To his dismay—although he was thoroughly chilled, he had not caught cold and was feeling fine—that is, physically. Before he opened the door, he quickly glanced into the front window. Sure enough, there sat his father reading in his armchair near the light of the window.

John walked in and with quavering voice announced, "I'm home."

His father laid down his book and peered over his glasses. "Well?"

John looked on the floor, saying nothing. (How would it sound if he had said, "I fell in love with a beautiful girl and couldn't bear to leave her.") So he simply stood there, staring at the tips of his father's shoes.

"Well?" his father repeated. "What do you have to say for yourself this time?"

"The Catletts were very kind to me. It was hard

to leave. We talked a lot about Mother. Mrs. Catlett asked all kinds of questions, they all did...and..." As John went into detail about his visit, his father listened with great interest.

It must have been the mention of his deceased first wife which softened his father's heart, so he was not nearly as angry as he had been in the past for similar offences.

"Can't you at least say you're sorry? I went to the trouble of asking my friend Joseph Manesty to get you a job. You had a great opportunity to make something of yourself in Jamaica. And what did you do—threw it away—just like that!" And he made an angry, descriptive gesture. "Now I have to make up some excuse as to why you did not appear! Don't you see the bad position it puts me in?"

His eyes downcast John simply said, "I am sorry, father." And for the moment he was truly contrite.

Picking up his book his father sighed, "Well, I'll have to try again somewhere." Then he looked over his son, "Your clothes are wet; better change and also get some hot tea."

With great relief John bounded up to his room on the second floor, and changed into dry clothing. Looking into the mirror, he pointed to his image and chortled, "Got by again, you lucky boy!"

The next day his father asked a captain friend to hire his son as a common sailor on a merchant ship bound for Venice. This time John couldn't wiggle out of it. As he was being assigned to his hammock, he thought, *There'll be no more sharing of the captain's cabin this time—no special treatment.* He made a face. *And I'll be just one of the sailors—which isn't saying much.*

He was quite aware that most of the sailors in those days were coarse, profane, illiterate, and usually downright wicked. Because of their low character, captains of ships were obliged to be very severe in order to maintain discipline, harshly punishing even slight misdemeanors. Moreover the food was poor, the pay low; but at least it was a job.

John soon discovered that this trip wasn't going to be a picnic and as always blamed his father. *So this is where he dumps me; on this rotten ship with these bums. I might have known it. Just like him.* As his anger increased, he began to take it out on everyone around.

Without the restraint of the presence of his father as on other trips, John abandoned all pretense at decency. He was going to show these bloody blokes who he was. If they were tough, he would be tougher. Profanity, ridicule of things sacred, licentiousness became his way of life.

When they anchored in Venice, he joined all the boys at the taverns, determined to gain a reputation with women, drink, and every kind of escapade. He knew he was superior intellectually to most of the sailors and wanted to prove he could also outdo them in sin.

But although he had deliberately pushed God out of his heart and life, God had not abandoned him. One night as he lay on his hammock, his head aching after a night of debauchery, he had a very disturbing dream: He was taking his turn at watch on deck, when an attractive Being came to him and gave him a ring.

"If you will preserve it carefully," he said, "you will be happy; if not, you will have only misery." And the man disappeared. As John pondered this, an evil-looking person approached him and by much reasoning persuaded John to toss the ring into the sea.

Immediately the sea turned ablaze, signifying the fires of hell. Amid his regrets, the first man reappeared, received John's words of contrition, dove in and retrieved the ring. When John eagerly reached for it, the man said, "I will keep it for you until you are ready."

This dream so troubled John that he could neither eat nor sleep for three days, and he amended his ways. But it soon wore off, and he returned to his sins.

The moment he returned from his voyage in December, 1743, his first thought was to spend Christmas with Mary. When John mentioned that, his father frowned. "Aren't you afraid you will make a nuisance of yourself by going there uninvited?" John thought so himself but to his father he replied, "I am sure they will not object." As he faced his father, John felt every muscle in his body tighten, and he braced himself for another verbal battle.

His father looked at him the way he always did—sternly. "Well John, I'll let you go (John thought, 'Who needs your permission?') on one condition—that you first let me arrange for another job."

John relaxed. So there wasn't going to be a battle. Good. "All right by me," he said with a shrug. And so the arrangement was made. John was to sail the first week of the new year.

After his father had introduced him to the captain of the new ship, he was informed of the sailing date. "And that means," his father said to John sternly, "that you must be back right after New Year's day. You hear?"

John did hear, but as so often in the past, did not obey and again stayed in Chatham until he knew the ship had sailed without him. His father was furious. "You're disgracing our good name! I've always been respected by my friends. And now everywhere I am getting to be known as the father of a worthless, lazy, cursing, insubordinate son." His father spat on the ground, his face contorted with rage. "I have a mind to disown you!"

While his father fumed, John stood stoically silent but inwardly spouting, *So go ahead and disown me. I don't mean anything to you anyway. Only one person ever loved me and that was Mother. And now there is another whose love I am determined to win.*

While his relationship with his father deteriorated, his romance did not fare much better. On his previous visits, the Catletts had been favorable. Mrs. Catlett even said, "When your mother was living, we had discussed the idea of you marrying some day." John was delighted to hear that. But as for Mary, she was either being coy or was not really interested in him.

But now, he could see that the Catletts themselves were changing toward him. As his visits to Chatham became more frequent, one day they took him aside and said, "We would like to have a frank talk with you concerning our daughter. We know that you are a fine person and would make a good husband for someone eventually. But really, your wages as a sailor would not be enough to support Mary properly."

John opened his mouth to protest, but Mrs. Catlett continued, "We also don't believe your temperament would be suited to that of our daughter. She is so cheerful and vivacious and you are...sort of heavy, you know; you don't say much...you two just wouldn't make a good pair."

John had been so immersed in his love for Mary that he hadn't even considered such practical matters as providing a living and having a good disposition. Wasn't love enough? Apparently not, according to the Catletts.

Would Mrs. Catlett ever stop talking! On and on she droned. "Of course, right now Mary is too young for marriage. Perhaps when your fortunes and disposition have improved, we would consider you—some time in the future. However, as things stand right now—we are sorry—but we will have to ask you not to come to our home any more, unless it be strictly at such a time when Mary would be absent."

John stared at them in disbelief. His face turned pale and he felt weak in the pit of his stomach. "You don't mean that! You can't! I love Mary deeply and would do everything to make her happy. I would live just for her."

"We are sorry," Mrs. Catlett repeated firmly, as she arose (her husband also arising), "but we have thought a lot about this and talked it over. This is our final word."

John searched the face of Mr. Catlett, hoping for some encouragement from him. But even though John sensed his sympathy and understanding, Mr. Catlett kept his eyes averted.

Crestfallen, John arose and slowly turned toward the barn to get his horse. On the way he looked longingly into the home, around the yard and garden, hoping for a glimpse of Mary. But she was nowhere around; very likely her parents had sent her away.

As he mounted his horse, he turned once again to look at the place in which his dreams had first begun and now had turned into a nightmare. Abruptly, he spurred his horse to a fast gallop. By the time he reached the woods some of his emotions had drained off. As he slowed down, memories crowded in.

The day when he had walked in the countryside with Mary, blissful in her presence.

"Mary," he had said, "you know that I love you with all my heart. There will never be anyone but you. Never. No matter where I am or what I am doing, you are in my thoughts. Tell me, Mary, you care for me, don't you, at least one little bit?"

Mary had smiled up at him, frankly, perhaps coquetishly. Then she fingered the lace of her dress and said, "I can't say 'yes,' and I can't say 'no'. I like you but don't love you. Besides I am not ready to think of marriage."

"I know that," John had pleaded, "we can talk marriage later; but it is love I am talking about now. Don't you, can't you..." He caught her hands and tried to get her to look at him.

"Don't do that," Mary had said, "somebody might see us and tell my parents. Besides, I don't know if I want you to hold my hands." And she pulled away.

Yet she was not really angry; she was smiling. *Oh, women, women,* John had thought later; *how can a man know what they are thinking and feeling?*

But what was the use of dreaming of what was past! He had gotten the word; he was not allowed to see Mary. As he slowly galloped on, his misery was so deep he felt he didn't care to live.

Not long after that, unable to bear it any longer and characteristically refusing to obey orders, he galloped right back to Chatham. Fortunately for him, Mary's parents happened to be away that afternoon. (But even if they had been there, he would still have made up some lie to justify his visit.)

Trembling with anticipation, he knocked on the door, and when Mary herself answered, he just stared, his eyes aglow with love, his heart pounding, his mouth dry. At first Mary looked surprised, then pleased. "Did you want something...."

"Mary," John broke in. "I've got to see you. Please come for a walk." To his delight she consented.

As they slowly walked toward a little wooded area John said, "Mary, your parents won't let me see you any more, but I..."

"I know," Mary said. "They told me."

"What do you think of it?" John was pleading, hoping

for a little encouragement.

"Well, perhaps they're right, perhaps not," she said coyly.

"But will you at least promise that you will write. Please. When I'm on trips?"

"You don't want me to disobey my parents, do you?" Her eyes were smiling.

"Please, please, Mary."

"We'll see," was all the answer he could get. But to his troubled heart, it seemed at least hopeful, since she didn't actually say "no."

And so they parted. As he galloped back on the now familiar road, his thoughts were gloomy. *Out of a job. Lost my girl. Father's displeased with me. Oh what misery, what woe!*

When he returned to London, he had no one in whom he could confide, no release for his bursting emotions. Certainly not his stepmother and most certainly not his father—who by now knew that many of his most recent escapades were on account of the girl. Because of this, the barrier between father and son had risen higher than ever before.

John slumped in a chair in his room trying to read, but all he could do was mope. The next day, restless and miserable, and for lack of anything else to do, despite the cold and gale winds, he hiked over to the nearest seaport. It was February 6, 1744.

For all his apparent reluctance to give himself to a sailor's life, he felt an attraction to the sea, to the seaport, to the sailors walking around in their blue-checked blouses. As he mingled with them, he felt a certain consolation in his anonymity. Nobody cared for him, and he didn't care for anybody there. He was just one other person milling around.

Through the door of a tavern he heard the sounds of laughter, male and female, and the clink of liquor glasses. He sauntered over.

Although he was not especially given to drink, he walked in, just to get out of the biting cold, sat at the bar and ordered rum. When he arose to go, a drunken sailor lurched against him, jarring him so that his hat fell off. John let loose a stream of profanity. "If you weren't so drunk, I'd beat you up." Then, noticing that he was attracting attention, he quickly walked out.

Utterly wretched, angry, churning with a variety of emotions, he walked aimlessly up and down the cobblestone streets, not really seeing anything—only Mary's face, Mary's smiling, teasing eyes, the strands of her light brown hair on her cheek.

He wandered back to the dock and looked at the Man-O-War anchored there, watched the sea gulls circle around, the tossing waves. Because the wild scene before him matched his mood, he felt a sort of kinship with it all, even deriving some comfort from it.

Suddenly, as he was musing, before he knew what was happening, several men surrounded him, pinned down his arms and dragged him—screaming, struggling, kicking, cursing—toward the wharf.

"What is going on here," he yelled through a volley of curses. Some tied his hands behind his back, pulled him to the edge of the dock and shoved him into a small boat. Bewildered at first—with a shock of horror he realized what was happening. He was being rowed to the HMS *Harwich*, a British navy ship, the Man-O-War.

He had been caught by the "press gang"!

eight

The HMS – The Royal Navy
England, 1744

OR SOME time, the British had been engaged in a cold war with France but now it looked as though the French fleets would attack any time. Britain beefed up its navy. Because of her widely flung empire, her navy was the world's greatest; so were the admirals and officers and captains—all superior men. But as for the crew, if the word "sailor" came to be synonymous with evil, it must have gotten that connotation in the early 18th century.

A job as sailor on a *merchant* ship attracted only the most intrepid and those whose toughness merited them a disregard for life. For merchant vessels in those days were often shipwrecked; or if they reached their destination, frequently many of the crew died because of hardships at sea, including poor food, harsh treatment, and the most undesirable accommodations. Mutiny and attempts at piracy were also not uncommon.

But if life on a merchant ship was bad, it was paradise

compared to a sailor's life in the Royal Navy. So bad in fact that in order to get enough of a crew to man the ships, prisoners were frequently offered their freedom if they would join the navy as common sailors.

And if there were still not enough sailors or when there was a loss of life through war or general sailing mishaps, then the "press gangs" took over. These were tough "recruiters" who prowled the quays or taverns seeking their prey. When they saw a good prospect, they sometimes dragged him into an alley, knocked him on the head or simply tied his hands and hustled him into small boats and rowed to the waiting navy ship.

And that is what happened to our hero. Captain Philip Carteret had sent out thirty-one recruiters who bagged eight men, one of them being Newton. As they bound the youth, he cursed and struggled fiercely. "Stop it! I'm the son of Captain Newton. Let me go!" John fumed. "My father will hear of this. Let me go or I'll kill you!" He struggled violently and swore profusely.

One of the men put his hand over John's mouth to stem the flow of profanity, saying, "My, my, what have we got here!"

After he had been aboard the ship a while, spent with rage and frustration, John yelled at the nearest officer, "You won't get a lick of work out of me; I'll not do a thing."

Archly, the officer replied, "We'll see about that. We have ways to make boys behave."

John shuddered. He knew about the irons, the leather cat-o-nine-tails, the dank prison, the solitude. He'd have to submit, he'd have to. *Oh curse the day I was born! Why did this ever happen to me?*

A huge, muscular sailor now roughly shoved him into a dimly lighted room, crowded with fifty other sailors. The stench of perspiration and human waste clinging to bodies and clothing seldom washed was nauseating. When John's eyes became accustomed to the dim light, he was horrified.

What kind of creatures are these? he thought. One of them looked evil enough to commit murder (and probably had); another sly as a fox, another bestial and stupid. A few looked intelligent but hard and cruel.

"So you joined the navy, eh," one of them laughed.

"I didn't join," John snarled; "the press gang got me."

"Ain't that too bad! What are you going to do about it, tell yore mama?" Every word was a filthy expression or curse so much worse than his that John was appalled.

After he had retreated into the hammock assigned to him, John lay there thinking, "So here I am. Stuck on this bloody navy ship. And France ready to declare war on us. Am I in deep trouble! I've got to get word to my father. He has to get me out of this mess."

Word did reach his father, but because war was so imminent, his father felt it was not the time to intercede for his son. So John stewed and raged for weeks, pronouncing curses on his father, the sailors, the officers, the British navy, and the God whose existence he denied.

But after about a month, his father sent word to John, "I have arranged with Captain Carteret to transfer you onto quarter deck as midshipman."

"Hooray," John shouted, almost beside himself with relief. "Good old father, bless his heart anyway. So now I will have the status of a sailor in training for a naval career. Great, just great!"

Immediately, he was assigned to new quarters with better food and accommodations and greatly improved general conditions. He was elated. Before long he began to strut before the common sailors, his former companions in misery, treating them with contempt, haughtily making disparaging remarks about their appearance and lack of intelligence. Now that he associated with midshipmen and officers, he was *somebody*.

One of the men with whom he now became very friendly was a gunner on the ship, very intelligent, loquacious, and a Freethinker. When he learned that John had read Lord Shaftesbury's *Characteristics* and *Rhapsody*, he began discussing the books with the youth. He found in John an interested listener, and one who obviously admired him as a thinker and philosopher.

By ridicule, shrewd argument, and quotations from Lord Shaftesbury, he daily seduced John, insisting that the only intelligent answer to all the questions of life and the universe was reason, not faith.

Up to this time—although John had been greatly influenced by Shaftesbury's books and was an unbeliever, he still unconsciously clung to a vague belief in God.

But his brand of religion never had amounted to much in the first place. Except for his brief periods of boyhood piety and the nearly two years of asceticism in his early teens, he had used religion basically as an escape from hell and a cloak for his sins.

Whatever remnants of religion that still clung to him from the influence of his mother were now too fragile to survive the subtle and persistent attacks of his Freethinking shipmate.

And so it was he who gave John the final push over the cliff into atheism. John completely turned his back on every remaining vestige of belief in God, heaven, hell, the devil, and the Bible. And he now boasted that he was a full-fledged Freethinker.

And so the ship's newest midshipman soon became known as a great blasphemer, twisting scripture and dramatizing biblical stories with so much humor that he had the whole crew roaring with laughter.

In December, 1744, the *Harwich* was preparing to sail to the East Indies. John had been in the captain's good graces, mostly because of his father's reputation; (certainly not by any good behavior or diligence or obedience to rules—in all of which his negative characteristics were soon apparent.)

On the other hand, John was intelligent and quickly grasped all that was required of him in his training as midshipman and so the Captain grudgingly admired him at least in this capacity and for the times when he did act responsibly.

One day John took the liberty of requesting a favor of the Captain. "May I have leave to go ashore for a few days to see the girl I plan to marry? After all, it will be five years before I see her again."

The captain looked at him uncertainly. "Well, John,

I've been lenient with you and given you permission before for supposedly short leaves and you have overstayed your time. What is it going to be this time?"

"I'm sorry, sir. I give you my word, it won't happen again. I promise to be back on time." When the captain looked at him dubiously, his lips were compressed. "Well, go ahead, I was young once and in love."

Totally ignoring the ban on his visit to Chatham, John gleefully left the ship, rented a horse and sped to his beloved. The Catletts didn't have the heart to send him away, so it was thrilling for him to spend the Christmas season with his Mary again.

During the next few days, John took every opportunity to be alone with her, pleading for a promise. "Mary, I'm going to be gone five years. I can't bear being separated from you for so long. Promise that you will keep yourself for me, please, Mary."

Mary looked at him coquettishly. "Oh no, John, I can't do that. After all, I might meet someone I like real well—some Prince Charming..."

"Perish the thought. That must never happen. Mary, I love you more than life. I will spend every moment making you happy, believe me."

Nothing he said changed her mind. "Then at least promise that you will write," he begged. "You can do me that little favor, can't you? Think of my lonely hours on that navy ship, of my misery away from you. If I got a letter from you at least now and then it would lighten my burden."

John's pleas finally extracted from Mary a reluctant

promise to write and with that he had to be content. A week flew by and John finally realized the Catletts were getting impatient and it was time to leave. It was not until he had said goodby and mounted his horse to return to the HMS *Harwich* that he began to think of facing the captain.

He was several days late when he clambered on board on New Year's day, 1745. "I'll have to explain to the captain...how could I stay just two days when I will be away from Mary for five years. Surely he will understand. *He* said he was young once and in love." With misgivings, he tried to convince himself.

When John reported to the captain, he met a very angry man. "So this is the way you keep your promises. I might have known it." The captain's voice was thick with contempt and anger. "John, this is the last time I will trust you. I have no respect for men of such low caliber."

The HMS *Harwich* finally joined a large fleet and sailed from Spithead where they had been anchored. They were on the seas only a short time when a storm suddenly blew up, so severe that several ships were lost. The next night the entire fleet was endangered by another storm on the coast of Cornwall. So the captain ordered the fleet to anchor at Plymouth to repair damages and wait out the storm.

It was while at Plymouth that John received word from his father. "I am in Tor Bay. I had invested in some of the ships that went down and am seeing to insurance. I now have an interest in the African company, trading in slaves."

John's hopes soared again. "So my father will be in Tor

Bay. I've got to see him. I'm going to beg him to get me off the *Harwich*. I'll tell him of the terrible dangers, how some of our fleet suffered in this awful storm, and it could have been our ship that went down. If I work on his sympathies maybe he will get me a job on the *African*. Surely he won't want me in the navy when we are on the brink of war. And certainly he didn't approve of my being press-ganged."

Characteristically, as soon as the idea entered his mind, he immediately acted on it, without thinking of consequences. To him, only the present was important, never the future. So he determined, "No matter what, I'm going to leave the *Harwich* before she sails out of Plymouth."

One day the captain (his anger apparently cooled) sent John in a boat to check on some of the men ashore to make sure none of them would desert. (Something which was commonly done among navy men, especially those who had been "pressed" into service.)

Even before he had reached shore in the small boat, John's plans were being made. "I'm going to desert. I refuse to remain in the navy. I didn't join; they forced me. I've got to see Father."

On shore he started off in a direction which he thought might lead toward Tor Bay, which was about forty kilometers distant. He walked very rapidly, partly because of the raw cold of March, but mostly to gain time. His mind was filled with happy thoughts. *The old gentleman will get me a job on his ship. Slave trading is good business. I'll soon get rich. Then I'll return to Chatham and with my fortunes improved, I'll be sure to get the consent of the*

Catletts. He whistled gaily as he strode along the high-way, his coat buttoned tightly, his scarf wrapped twice around his neck. At nightfall he kept plunging toward his destination. Sleep was out of the question.

After a full day and part of the next day, he figured that in another two hours he would reach Tor Bay. He was brimming with good cheer and high expectations as he ran up the crest of a little hill—when his heart nearly stopped beating at what he saw. "No, it can't be!" he cried. Frantically, he looked from side to side; there was only open field, no woods in which to flee and hide. The small company of soldiers quickly galloped forward and surrounded him.

"Halt!" one of them shouted. "Who are you and where are you going?" At first John wanted to say, "You've got to let me go; I'm the son of Captain Newton," but realizing the folly of such answer, he simply replied, "I'm John Newton."

"That's him, the deserter from the *Harwich*," said one of the soldiers, pointing dramatically. "He fits the description." Then he fingered his gun. "Don't try to escape. It will make your punishment that much harder."

Gloomily, John lept on the back of the horse behind one of the soldiers, too numb to even attempt explanations. What would they think if he had said he wanted to see his father to get him out of the navy? So in silence he rode along with the soldiers until they reached Plymouth.

There he was told to dismount and with a soldier on each side was escorted through the streets. Everywhere people turned to stare. "I know what they're thinking,"

John mused, "that I'm a common thief or criminal. I'm not, I am...oh what's the use, I'm a deserter from the British navy and got caught."

His face burned with shame. At first he thought of proudly holding his head high, but realized how foolish such defiance would look, so he let his shoulders sag and his head hang into his sunken chest.

Not far from where the ship was anchored, he was placed in the guardhouse on bread and water, where he fumed for two days. Then he was rowed to the HMS *Harwich*. The captain was waiting. There was no mercy on his face, only anger and disdain. "So this is my trusted midshipman! I send you to watch out for deserters and you become one yourself! How noble, how patriotic!" He spat on the deck. "You scum!" He nodded to one of the officers near by. "Put him in irons."

nine

The Transfer

FOR TWO days John lay in the small dank prison room of the ship, cursing and raging. He cursed the captain, the crew, God and fate. Limp and frustrated, he stared at the ceiling, his mind a blank. Finally the door opened, and he saw outlined in the doorway two tall, tough-looking men. When they came near, he noted cruel eyes looking at him impassively, then felt an iron grip as they jerked him to his feet, shoved him up the ladder onto the deck.

John strove not to show his terror, taking deep breaths to still the pounding of his heart. He tightened every muscle, hardened his heart in preparation for his ordeal. He knew what was coming, having seen it before. With rebellion and hatred seething within, he glared at the men assembled.

There he saw standing in a circle the Captain, the officers (including his former companions, the other midshipmen) and the 350 common sailors. In the eyes of some of the midshipmen he saw pity; on the faces of most of the common sailors only tight-lipped animosity. The Captain himself seemed made of stone. He looked at John with cold eyes then ordered sharply, "Stand forward."

John complied.

The captain then repeated the crime: "Deserted from the navy, His Majesty's Ship, the *Harwich*." He then turned to the Master at Arms and ordered: "Strip him and seize him up."

The Master at Arms conducted John to a grating to which his feet were tied. Then he stripped John to the waist, after which he made him lean over another grating in front of him, lashing the youth's wrists to it.

"Give him the first dozen." ordered the captain.

A boatswain's mate stepped forward, grasped the cat-o-nine-tails with both hands, lifted it over his head and with great force swished it through the air onto John's back twelve times. At each thud John writhed in pain, but refused to let a word escape from his lips. What did come from between his gritted teeth were hissed curses at the assembled men. Defiance and hatred and pain distorted his face into sheer ugliness.

Angered at the continued rebellion John displayed, the captain shouted, "Give him the next dozen." Now another boatswain took his place and administered his dozen. He was followed by others, each administering a dozen lashes.

Repeatedly, the thongs cut through the air. John felt blood run down his naked back and into his shoes; saw blood spattered on the grill and floor. The pain, the pain—

it was getting unbearable. Just before he had received the last of his hundred lashes, his curses became weaker and weaker, his defiance broke and as he began to slip into unconsciousness, he faintly heard the captain call, "Pipe down."

As a sailor cut the ropes which bound his hands and feet, John collapsed onto the pool of his own blood. With great effort he drew himself to his knees. His hands were slippery with blood and as he tried to pull himself up by holding onto the grating, several times his grasp slipped and he sprawled on the deck. Humiliated and furious, he averted his eyes from the circle of observers. Oh how he hated them, every one of them!

When he was finally able to rise, he wiped his bloody hands on his trousers, then collapsed, face down on the deck. Two sailors now stepped forward, threw a cloth over John's lacerated back and carried him down below to the cockpit—the place reserved for the wounded in time of war.

He lay on a cot in too great agony to care whether he lived or died. And then he saw the door open and the ship's physician came in to tend to his wounds. John was surprised at the kindness with which the physician treated him, and responded with grateful looks. Oh, how he suffered! His back felt like a piece of raw meat, swollen and exquisitely tender and painful.

It was only the daily ministrations of the physician which made life bearable. After a week, the doctor said, "Young man, you are doing very well and will soon be released."

"Thank you sir," John replied; "you have been very

kind."

The day the doctor pronounced him recovered, a deep gloom settled over John. Now what would happen? He had a horrible suspicion of what it would be and recoiled when the Master at Arms entered.

"You will now receive the second part of your punishment," he said crisply. "You are being deprived of your rank and will return to your former quarters."

The words fell like blows, far worse than those he had received physically. For a moment John stared into the impassive eyes of the officer, then closed his eyes and moaned, "Oh no, oh no!"

He arose and followed the man as he escorted him to the quarters of the common sailors.

John flopped down on his hammock and shut his eyes. What were those sounds from the hammocks all around? Was it laughter, scorn, hissing, cursing? It came from the men who he had so haughtily scorned as beneath him while he was consorting with the captain and officers as midshipman. Now he was again one of the formerly despised sailors, and they made the most of his humiliation.

"Serves you right! Acting so proud and smart when you was on quarter deck. Now you take your own medicine. You'll get no pity from us, sailor." The other men yelled in agreement, "That's right; you're telling it right!"

John had nothing to say so kept quiet, swallowing his pride. This public disgrace and degradation had wounded his spirit deeply. He had lost his rank as midshipman; now he was mocked by the lowest of the common sailors.

He had lost the friendship of the other men in training, the respect of the captain and officers. And worst of all by far, he feared he had lost his opportunity to win Mary. "I am finished," he mourned. "She is going to hear about this and will hate me. Her parents will never, never let me even come anywhere near her now."

Yet despite his terrible sufferings, he never once attempted to call on the Lord. God was completely out of his life and thoughts, simply non-existent. And so he suffered alone, without human or divine consolation.

As he brooded over his state, not willing to accept his own guilt, he decided it was all the captain's fault. "He surely could have overlooked such a little thing as deserting, especially since I had been forced into the navy. I'm going to kill him; he ruined my life!" Enraged, he planned revenge. "Maybe knife him or push him into the sea. Of course, if I did that, I would have to jump in after him.

"Or maybe I should forget about killing him. Word might reach Mary that I had become a murderer. And I want my memory to be pleasant to her. No, I can't commit murder. I'll just leap overboard; no one would know it was deliberate. I could make it look like an accident. Then Mary would at least have some compassion for me."

As the days wore on, John abandoned all thoughts of murder and suicide and tried to reconcile himself to the hardships of life as a common sailor.

"I'll be on this bloody ship for five years," he lamented; "I'll never see Mary again. She will be married before I ever return to England." His gloom was so deep that he hardly cared to eat or talk; he hated everybody. He knew no one cared for him, so he just kept to himself, performing his duties morosely, and returning to his hammock as soon as possible.

The ship sailed from Plymouth to Madeira where it remained for several weeks. John knew from talk he overheard that business matters were completed, and they would sail to India the next day.

Unknown to him, he was again to experience another act of Providence which would change the course of his life.

On that morning he had no particular duties so he lay in his hammock. While there, one of his former companions, a midshipman, came down and half in jest, half seriously said, "Get up, old man. You can't sleep all day." John simply grunted and turned over.

Suddenly, the midshipman whipped out his knife and with one quick slash cut down the hammock and scampered off laughing hilariously. John landed on the deck with a thud and as he scrambled to his feet, directed a stream of profanity in the direction of the departing midshipman. He was furious, but helpless to retaliate. But now that he was fully awake, he dressed.

For lack of anything else to do, he went up on deck. As he aimlessly glanced to his right, he noticed a sailor putting a small bundle into a little boat which was bobbing at the ship's side. Immediately his lethargy vanished and his heart began pounding with excitement. "What's he doing that for?" he asked an officer, pointing to the sailor.

The officer indicated a nearby vessel anchored, a Guinea ship. "They're making a trade. Two men from the Guinea ship are being exchanged for two from this ship." (A common practice.)

Alive with hope, John begged the officer, "Please, sir, hold that boat a moment." Looking somewhat surprised, the officer complied. Newton ran to the Lieutenant. "Oh sir, I beg of you, please ask the captain to give me permission to be one of the men to go on the Guinea ship. Oh I beg of you, please ask him." He looked at the officer so earnestly, his eyes so pleading that the lieutenant went to the captain with the message. "Tell him I'll be eternally grateful," John called after him.

John didn't know why it happened—perhaps because he had given the captain so much trouble by his wretched conduct, his arrogance, his insubordination, his overstaying so many leaves—that the captain was glad to get rid of him. At any rate, the captain snapped, "Let him go."

In a moment the lieutenant returned with the message, "The captain gives you permission to transfer to the Guinea ship."

"Oh thank you sir, thank you," John cried. He rushed down into the lower deck, grabbed his few belongings, including his one book, Barrow's *Euclid*, and in a few minutes leaped into the boat with the other sailor. While in the boat, he was so excited and overjoyed that he looked at his companions, smiled and shook his head, "I can't believe it; I can't believe it!"

(Years later, in looking back over the incident, John was

awed by this act of Providence. For in less than half an hour, and in a way which seemed miraculous, the direction of his life was moved one step farther into God's purposes.)

ten

—

The Guinea Snow Pegasus

As THEY were bobbing over the waves to the *Guinea Snow Pegasus*, John's excitement grew. "I am free, free, after my misery on that stinking Man-O-War. Free from the humiliation of my whipping and emotion. Free to be and do what I please!"

To him, freedom from restraint was the big thing. While he was on the HMS *Harwich*, he was far from angelic, but he had actually been keeping in check the worst of the evil that surged within. "Now at last I will be myself," he exulted. "I will say what I feel, do what I please; give full reign to my impulses."

In a few minutes John and his companion clambered on the *Guinea*, smiling and on their best behavior toward the officer who greeted them. "Welcome aboard," he said, "I hope you will enjoy your stay with us."

"Thank you," John replied, "I am sure we will."

After they had conversed a while, John learned that this was a merchant ship engaged in the slave trade. "Oh," exclaimed John, "my father was also engaged in the slave trade, as captain of the *African*." For days he chaffed under his self-imposed good behavior, finding it more and more difficult especially to control his tongue. One day a sailor accidentally bumped into him so hard that John staggered backward and would have fallen except that he grabbed a rope. "Watch where you are going you idiot. I have a mind to blacken your eyes," he shouted.

Surprised and angry, the sailor doubled his fists for a fight, advancing menacingly toward John. It was only the appearance of an officer which prevented a brawl. But John kept up the stream of foul words in the presence of the officer.

"What's going on here, John," the officer asked, his eyebrows raised.

"Nothing, nothing," John said as he attempted to cool his anger.

This episode seemed to have opened the floodgates of John's real personality and from then on he revealed what he really was. Increasingly, he was inclined toward indolence or disobeying orders or following them in his own way. In addition he began openly to ridicule God and religion, deliberately misquoting scripture and making blasphemous jokes about sacred things—setting the common sailors to coarse laughter.

After a month of hearing these reports, Captain Penrose approached John, his face severe. "Newton, I have been receiving disturbing information about your conduct and attitudes and am surprised. I had the notion that the son of Captain Newton would be as decent and dependable as the father."

Startled and insulted, John was ready with a quick retort but instead fumbled with his words. "Why, sir, I don't know what you are talking about. I...."

Curtly, the captain replied, "I am sure you know exactly what I mean." And he strode away.

Stung by the captain's rebuke, John determined to get revenge, so he composed a clever song in which he ridiculed the captain and his ship (not mentioning names but making it obvious who was meant.) Then he taught it to the sailors. When they had been drinking enough to obscure their better judgment, the sailors would sing it loudly, accompanied by raucous laughter.

This of course brought John into more disfavor with the captain and officers. The captain, although not professing religion was particularly displeased with John's blasphemous jokes.

One day as John was entertaining the sailors with a mimic of the feeding of the five thousand, the captain heard of it and confronted him. "This is blasphemy. Stop it, or you'll bring God's wrath upon this whole crew." "God," scoffed Newton, "oh come on now, only women and fools believe such nonsense. This is the Age of Reason."

Angrily, the captain shook his head, "I don't care what age it is. Stop this, you hear. You are influencing the whole crew to your way of thinking and doing."

"Good, that's exactly what I aim to do," Newton retorted insolently.

"Young man," the captain exclaimed, "if we weren't

so short-handed and if I didn't respect your father, I would ship you off onto the next Man-O-War that comes around. They know how to tame the likes of you." Glaring at John the captain abruptly turned on his heel and left.

Subdued by the threat John said nothing more and sullenly went off to his duties. To be returned to a Man-O-War was the last thing he wanted. He had had enough of that!

Not long after this incident the captain suddenly became ill and died. During the burial at sea, Newton kept casting furtive glances at the first mate, the next in line to take command. "Now I'm going to get it," John worried. "I've lost favor with all of the officers. How will I ever get out of this one?"

That night as he lay in his hammock brooding over his future, terrorized by the fear of being returned to the Man-O-War, he thought, *I've got to figure a way to get out of this mess.* Frantically, he thought of one thing after another. After a half hour of mental torment, he remembered Claw, who was one-fourth owner of the *Guinea* and who had made a fortune selling slaves. He was on this ship returning from England and was now going ashore for more slaves.

I've got it! I'm going to persuade Claw to hire me! Jubilant at this idea and greatly relieved, John immediately fell asleep. The next morning he approached Claw. "Sir, I know I have not always been what you would call an exemplary sailor. But I know how to do a good day's work and promise that if you hire me, I will be a valuable helper."

Claw fixed his eyes on the youth, looking him over thoroughly. Finally he said, "I could always use an extra hand. You look pretty sturdy. How old are you?"

"Nineteen, sir."

"Mature enough to be responsible. I believe you can do a good job if you have a mind to. Are you in good health?"

"Excellent health, sir."

"Then you're hired."

"Thank you, sir, I'll do my best to please you." Elated, he hurried to the first mate who was now captain and begged for a discharge. To John's delight, it was granted at once. (Apparently, the new captain had had enough of John's kind of service and actions!)

As the *Guinea* sailed along the east coast of Africa, John again began his dreams. *I'm going to get rich like Claw. It will probably take a year or so. And then I'll return to England and claim my beloved.* He sighed happily.

During all of his hardships on the HMS *Harwich* and his careless and dissolute life on the *Guinea*, Mary had not once left his thoughts. As he lay on his hammock thinking, as he stood on the deck at night, looking into the star-studded sky, his thoughts constantly turned to Mary.

He pictured her as he last saw her—the sun shining on her light brown hair, the vivacious smile, the charm, her demureness and yet sparkling liveliness; her lovely form, the glow of her fair skin. How could he ever forget her!

And now that he was going to work with Claw and get rich, his dreams would come true!

eleven

The Plantane Islands

/N THE morning as they neared shore, John stood beside Mr. Claw and looked ahead as his new master pointed. "Over there is where we're heading—the Plantane Islands, two miles off the mainland of Sierra Leone. There's three islands, and we'll settle on the biggest. It's low and sandy, lots of palm trees and a nice sheltered cove, fine for landing the small boats we use in trading."

John had already learned while on the *Guinea* slave ship the method by which slaves were obtained. Some of the more enterprising Africans would raid villages of enemy tribes and capture men, women and children. They took their victims to the coast to sell to English and American slave traders who waited in their ships. The African traders received payment in household utensils, knives, beads, liquor, shells, gunpowder.

The slaves were shackled and packed into ships like animals. Many died before they reached their destinations. The healthiest and best looking were sold for the highest price. The most attractive women were often sexually used by officers and crew.

In the 17th and 18th centuries, no one thought anything wrong with the trade, since they considered the natives to be sub-human heathens who would benefit by their contacts with "Christian" white men. John Newton of course shared this common viewpoint.

As they neared the island, Claw informed John, "We'll build you a house over there; then I'll take you with me in a small boat on inland trips up the river to get slaves."

"That is fine with me, sir, and I promise to serve you well." (John was of course thinking of the wages he would receive.)

When they landed, Newton discovered that Claw had a house occupied by PI, a prominent native woman with whom he lived as his wife—a common practice among white traders. Claw also had a number of black slave servants living in nearby quarters. Besides the convenience of having a mistress and housekeeper, Claw valued PI for her influence among the natives in his slave business deals.

PI was a buxom, rather attractive woman, flashily dressed in European style, heavily adorned with beads. As she greeted Claw affectionately, John looked away in embarrassment. Claw turned to John. "Oh by the way, this is PI."

PI greeted him with a big smile which John instinctively felt was false—the coldness in her eyes betrayed her real feelings. As he ate with Claw and PI, John noted that the table was elaborately set with European china and silver. During the meal he also noticed an unconcealed look of displeasure on PI's face as he and Claw discussed business matters. Apparently, she wanted all of Claw's attention.

That night as John retired, he thought about PI's coldness and realized with a shock, *PI is jealous of me. She resents Claw giving me attention. Looks like I'm in for trouble with her.*

He had been on the island only a few days when he became so ill that Claw had to leave him and go inland alone. "PI," he said to his mistress, "John's taken jungle fever. Would you mind taking care of him until he gets over it? I'll be back as soon as I finish my business."

"I surely will, my dear," smiled PI.

Whether or not she meant it, John never knew. At first she did take good care of him, supplying him with cool water and food. But after a week, since his fever continued, she must have grown weary of nursing care and began to shamefully neglect him. After all, he meant nothing to her except a rival for Claw's attention.

For days John lay on a mat spread on the ground, with a log for a pillow. The little hut afforded no shelter from the hot sun, which made his burning fever and pounding headache that much worse.

One night as he lay suffering, longing for food and water, he heard a faint rustle near his bed. It was one of the slaves, a servant of PI's. The man put his finger to his lips, indicating silence, then offered him water and a little food from his own meager rations, silently slipping away into the darkness before he should be discovered. Oh how grateful John was, and yet how humiliated that he should be ministered to by a slave.

One day PI walked into his hut carrying a plate of remains of her feast. John's pride was by now so greatly humbled and he was so starved that he eagerly reached for the dish. But because he was so weak he dropped the plate and the food scattered all over the floor. To John it was a tragedy but PI went off laughing hilariously—not bothering to replace the food.

How John hated her! Hated her for humiliating him for treating him worse than one of her slaves. This was far more degrading than his whipping and demotion on the *Harwich*.

As he lay in his hut recovering, he raged at his fate, his helplessness. Life was giving him a raw deal and he responded by hardening his heart still more.

Gradually he got better, but was still so weak he could hardly walk. Once PI shouted, "Get up, you worthless, good-for-nothing. You're not sick. You're just lazy. You don't even earn your food." John didn't dare express the anger and contempt he felt, lest it should provoke more ill-treatment. So he swallowed his pride and said nothing. When he was finally able to stand on wobbly legs, PI told her servants to mimic his walk and to throw limes at him. Some even threw stones but she did not reprove them, instead laughed at his misery.

Bitterness arose within him so strongly that he felt as though if he had the strength he would have struck her, but he dared not. When Claw returned from his trip Newton told him of PI's treatment, but she denied it and he believed her.

As soon as John was sufficiently recovered, Claw took him on his first inland trip. All went well and Claw said, "I see you are a good worker. We will get along fine as long as you keep this up." He looked pleased and slapped John on the back. From then on they had a good relationship and enjoyed each other's company.

But after the second trip Claw confronted Newton, "What's this I hear about you? A fellow tradesman said that while I was away you stole some of my goods and hid them."

John's mouth dropped open. Indignantly he cried, "That's a lie. A great big lie. I never stole anything. I am not and never have been a thief. Search my quarters. You won't find anything. I've done a lot of rotten things in my life, but stealing isn't one of my vices. Believe me, Mr. Claw, I am telling the truth."

But Claw didn't believe him, so from then on when he was away on a trip he chained John on the boat, leaving less than a pint of rice for one day's allowance. If he stayed longer, John had nothing to eat. Sometimes he was given the entrails of a chicken PI had prepared for Claw, which John used as bait. When the current was still, he caught a fish or two. This he broiled or half burned, but it was delicious to him, and he ate it with great relish.

He would be exposed for twenty to forty hours in rain and strong winds without any shelter. His only clothing was his trousers, a kerchief for his head and a piece of cotton cloth for his shoulders.

Under this treatment from both Claw and PI his haughty and rebellious spirit was so broken, he hardly seemed like the same person. (In all of this, unknown to him, God was at work, taking down his pride.)

When he was finally allowed to go ashore, he would often sit in a sandy cave or on the shore of some remote part of the island with the one book which he carried with him—Barrow's *Euclid*. In his misery and loneliness, this book was his only consolation and diversion. He would pass away the time by giving his mind to mathematical studies, tracing the diagrams on the shore with a long stick. In this way he mastered the six books of *Euclid*. It was his one way of keeping his mind occupied to maintain his sanity. The only other thought he had, and always in the background, was that of Mary—like a sad and woeful dirge.

Although Claw continued to take John along on inland trips to get slaves, their once good relationship was destroyed because he remained suspicious.

During a lull in their trading, John was given the task of planting young lime trees. As he bent over in the hot sun setting the young plants, Claw and his mistress walked by. Sarcastically, Claw remarked to John:

"Who knows. By the time these plants grow into trees and bear fruit, you may be back in England and get to be captain of a ship and come back to eat the limes of these very trees."

Newton lifted his head and looked at Claw and PI standing there, having a laugh at his expense.

"If that is a prophecy," Newton retorted, "I will give you another. If I ever get back to England, I will become king of Poland." And he returned to his task.

twelve

Going Native

WHILE ON the island, Newton wrote several letters to his father telling of his wretched condition; he also wrote to Mary, pouring out his love to her, begging her to wait for his return. These letters were taken aboard the latest passing ship and entrusted with the captain to deliver whenever they reached England, which could be a matter of several years.

When John wrote his father he was not particularly interested in seeing him; his only thought was of Mary. (John discovered later that upon hearing of his son's distress, his father had contacted his friend Joseph Manesty in Liverpool and had asked: "If you ever have a ship in the vicinity of Sierra Leone, please instruct its captain to look up my son on the Plantane Islands and bring him back to England." (And Mr. Manesty had kindly consented.)

One day Claw surprised John by saying, "I know a man

who lives on the other side of the island—Williams by name—he has several factories in different locations and could use a smart young man like you. How would you like that?"

Unbelievingly, John stared at Claw for a moment, then replied, "That sounds very interesting." Then he hesitated. "Mr. Claw, you haven't paid me yet for all the time I have been working for you."

"Pay! When you asked me to take you on, we didn't have any agreement about pay."

"But I just took it for granted," said John.

"That doesn't mean anything. You have nothing in writing. I considered you as, sort of my slave, or let's say my apprentice. You learned a lot about the slave trade working for me. That's worth something."

John was so furious he was ready to strike Claw, but his mind quickly went into gear. *I'd better stay on good terms with Claw or else lose my chance with this Mr. Williams.* So all he said was, "If that's the way you look at it...All right, let's go to see Mr. Williams."

As the two men trudged over the sandy ground of the island to the other side, John was thinking, wondering what was in store for him now. Would it be more misery under a new master, or would he have better luck?

But why is Claw suddenly letting me go, he thought. *Is he afraid he will get in trouble for treating me like a slave, working without pay?* Whatever Claw's motive, John was about to begin a new chapter.

When they reached the other end of the island, John saw

a well-built home and neatly kept yard. Williams was sitting on the front Veranda. Claw introduced the two and left, saying, "Mr. Williams, you will find that John is an intelligent, hard-working man. You will be satisfied with him."

Mr. Williams had five factories in distant locations with white men in charge. One day after John had been working there for a few months, Williams said, "John, I see you are very capable and dependable. How would you like a share in the management of one of my factories, with another man?"

Trying to hide his delight and surprise, John said, "Mr. Williams, I would be pleased. And I know you will not regret your confidence in me." Apparently, Mr. Williams did not, for he placed more and more responsibilities upon his newest employee, entrusting him with large sums of money.

Life became easy and pleasant. He had all the good food he wanted, good wages, women on demand, pleasures limited only by his surroundings.

By now John was definitely a changed person. His sufferings and humiliations had broken his proud, rebellious spirit and self-will. He had also abandoned his indolent and independent ways and had become diligent and hardworking. He became so content in this new lifestyle that unconsciously he was beginning to "go native." This was an expression used when a white man working in Africa gradually became assimilated into the culture of the natives. Had he continued, he would have taken a native mistress as Claw did and settled in Africa for life.

One afternoon as John walked alone on the shore, he realized this infatuation was growing upon him, and he became disturbed. *But what's the use of trying to stop it? There's nothing for me in England. My stepmother doesn't want me; my father doesn't care. Mary has no doubt married by now. So why should I return? Might as well go native and remain here.* With a mingling of despair and resignation, he shrugged his shoulders and began walking back to his quarters.

It had now been fifteen months since having come to the Plantanes and life had fallen into a routine. Meanwhile, the *Greyhound*, the ship which Mr. Manesty dispatched on business with the request that its captain look for John Newton when they arrived in Sierra Leone, was nearby. The captain inquired about Newton but when he learned that he no longer lived with Claw and that he was working for Williams was inclined to forget about his promise to Manesty to find the young man. He stayed only a few hours, not bothering to look up Williams on the far end of the island, as he was anxious to get on with his journey.

But that day in February, 1747, it "happened" that Mr. Williams had sent John and another worker on business to Kittam, which was about 100 miles away. It also "happened" that Kittam was only a mile from the seacoast.

Because Newton was short of supplies for barter, he asked his partner to go to the seashore on the chance that a vessel might be passing by. The custom in those days was that the person on shore would make a smoke signal in token of a desire to trade.

Newton's partner soon reached the shore, and as he scanned the horizon was happy to see a ship in the distance. He built a fire and made the smoke signal.

Neither he nor John Newton of course knew how providential this whole incident was. For if the two men had been in this particular location just half an hour later, the ship would have sailed out of reach. Furthermore, if they had been at any of the other four factories belonging to Williams they would have been away from the seashore. So in God's appointment, the *Greyhound* saw the signal and came to anchor.

John's companion took a canoe to the ship. At once one of the officers asked, "By the way, we are looking for a young man named John Newton. He is supposed to be somewhere on the Plantanes. Do you happen to know where we could locate him?"

Surprised, the man replied, "I sure can. We work together for Mr. Williams. He's on the Plantanes but it just happens that we are in Kittam on business. He is just a little way from where we are now."

When word reached the captain of the *Greyhound*, he at once came ashore to personally deliver his message. After greetings, the captain said to John, "I have a message for you from your father. He has received your letters of distress, and I am now here to take you back to England."

John stood silent for a while, then said, "Well, sir, I had

been in deep distress while working for Mr. Claw, but with Mr. Williams everything has changed. I appreciate my father's interest and also your kindness in taking the trouble to look me up. But I am very well situated now, working for Williams, in charge of one of his factories, doing very well financially...And Africa really isn't such a bad place to live...other white men have settled here for life."

The captain was disturbed. "But your father begged that you return...and besides..."(And here John learned later that the captain began to fabricate stories)... "and besides, I have quite a packet of letters and papers for you on the ship. I didn't take them along, thinking you were surely coming with me."

At this, John's heart began to pound. He had written to Mary—perhaps there was a letter from her. And as he looked at the captain, his interest suddenly revived. And yet, John thought, *Surely not; she must be married by now. I couldn't stand the disappointment to find that out...*

As John hesitated, the captain told what John later discovered was another tale: "I also have more good news; your father said that a relative of yours died and left you an inheritance of 400 pounds a year."

Suspiciously John looked at the captain, but he did remember an aged relative who might have died and left him something. Suddenly this talk of England opened that compartment within his heart where he had buried all his thoughts of Mary...and the great longing to see her welled up (perhaps she wasn't married, perhaps...). With the money he had earned working for Williams and with this inheritance, he would now be an acceptable suitor for Mary. And if she was married he could always return to Kittam, spend the rest of his life working for Williams and bury himself in Africa.

As he began to change his attitude toward the captain's pleas, the captain made one more promise: "I promise you that if you come aboard you will share my cabin, be my companion and won't have to do a lick of work. How's that for a deal?"

With that, John's reluctance dissolved and the weight of the whole fifteen months of misery, captivity, loneliness, and despair dropped off, and he felt like a freed slave.

"Yes, sir," he said, "I'll come aboard. I'll be glad to. Now if you will just give me time to get my belongings and earnings, I'll be right with you." In a few hours he stood on the deck of the *Greyhound*, watching the shore of Kittam disappear in the distance.

thirteen

The Greyhound
The Year 1748

NOT MANY minutes after John was on board the *Greyhound*, he approached Captain Swanwich. "And now, may I have the packet of letters, please?" Eagerly, he stretched out his hand.

The captain hemmed and hawed, turned red and finally blurted, "Well, you see, Mr. Manesty said your father was so anxious to have you back in England, that he practically ordered me to do just about anything to get you on board. And so I...well, since you didn't seem too anxious to come...I just had to...fabricate a little."

John stared incredulously. "You mean you don't have any letters for me at all?" He was speechless for a long moment, then, "That was a low, low trick you played on me, Sir, a low trick...And I suppose the inheritance talk was a fable too?"

"Well, yes, as a matter of fact, it is. Curses, why did I ever get involved in this anyway?" Then he tried to look pleasant. "But what I said about your sharing my cabin and not having to work is of course true; I mean, that is how it will be."

Out of respect for the office of the man as captain, John repressed any further anger and simply said, "Thank you, sir, I appreciate this favor."

Having settled this matter, the captain took John around to the various officers and introduced him as "the son of Captain Newton, who is a good friend of Joseph Manesty." This of course gave John the status which he relished and soothed the remnants of his anger.

That night as he lay on a comfortable bunk in the captain's cabin, the two men conversed in the dark.

"What's this ship dealing with?" John asked.

"Gold, ivory, dyer's wood, beeswax. This cargo takes much longer to accumulate than slaves. We've been in Gambia about five months already and still have a long way to go. Tomorrow we range the whole coast as far south as Cape Lopez."

"Where is that located?"

"It's one degree south of the equinoctial. When we get there, you'll be far from home, actually a thousand miles farther than when you were in the Plantanes. We'll be stopping at various places to pick up merchandise. But remember, I promised you that you don't have to work, so don't worry about that."

"That will be a relief, after working so hard on the island."

The men talked awhile longer, then fell asleep. The next day John sauntered around the ship getting more acquainted with the officers, trying to fit his behavior into that of the men he now associated with.

Since he had nothing to do, he soon became restless. Sometimes he kept his mind occupied by working on his mathematics. At times he picked up *Thomas à Kempis*, a devotional book he found in the captain's library. He read it just for diversion, not having any interest whatsoever in its spiritual content. But that also became tiresome.

After a month of good conduct, one day he had a disagreement with an officer and suddenly exploded: "You always think you are so right! You never listen to someone else's opinion." And in his profanity, he frequently used God's name in vain.

The officer looked at him in surprise. "Well, what's this? The angel suddenly loses his wings and dons horns! And such horns!"

In the mood for a verbal battle, John retorted, "I hope you're not stupid enough to believe such nonsense as believing in devils or angels." And he began to dance, waving his arms acting like an angel.

"Look, I'm an angel, so sweet and beautiful." And suddenly he changed his expression, "Look out, angel, here comes the devil," and he pretended to plunge a pitchfork at the angel.

By now a number of the sailors had gathered and joined the hilarious laughter—which was just what John liked. From that time he continued to entertain the crew with blasphemous ridicule of things sacred. Nothing was spared—neither churches nor preachers nor scripture, not even God Himself. He actually spent time now looking into the Bible he found in the library, seeking passages suitable for blasphemous mimicry. He debased his creative mind in devising clever skits.

One day when the sailors were drinking rum, John passed his hands over the cups and muttered, "Hocus, pocus, let this rum be changed into wine." He rolled his eyes upward and assumed a devout expression, to the great amusement of his audience.

After a few months of this, the captain approached John solemnly, "John, I hear you have been carrying on in ways that are offensive."

"What do you mean 'offensive'?" John bristled.

The captain, a man of short temper, suddenly flared, "You know what I mean. You have a terribly foul mouth and can out-curse the worst of my sailors. I'm not saying anything about that. But I don't like the way you are making fun of religion. It just isn't right."

"Well, so what have we got here?" John said sarcastically. "Maybe you should have been a preacher instead of a sailor." And he walked away angrily, thinking, *Is my freedom of self-expression again to be restricted? Why are people always trying to put me in a straitjacket? Why can't I do and say as I please?*

Since the captain and John shared the cabin, there now arose a coolness between the two. One day when John had been particularly obnoxious, the captain reproved him severely. "John, I'm almost sorry I took you on board. We have been having some bad luck lately, and I wouldn't doubt but that it is because we have a Jonah on board."

"Oh come now," John cried. "Don't tell me that you believe that yarn—on top of all the other foolishness in that book of fables."

"I'm not saying whether I believe it or not," replied the captain. "I'm not a religious man and don't expect to be one. But you are carrying your kind of jokes too far. You are having a bad influence on the others as well."

"Isn't that sad," John retorted. "I should think that the captain and his officers would be intelligent enough not to be disturbed. As for the sailors, what's wrong with my entertaining them? Everybody enjoys a good laugh."

"One of these days God will punish you for your blasphemies," said the captain.

It was not long before this "prophecy" nearly came true, and who is to say whether God was punishing him or the devil trying to take him?

One night while the *Greyhound* sailed on the River Gabon, John became bored and seeking diversion, he rounded up five of the sailors and suggested, "Let's have a drinking contest, boys. See who can hold the most."

He grabbed a large shell, filled it with rum and proposed a toast. "May the good and blessed devil take the winner and may the sweet and lovely angels get drunk with us."

As he gulped down the rum, the men joined in the contest, each trying to outdo the other. However, although John had committed every sin in the books, he was never much of a drinker so his brain reacted negatively. He soon became so inflamed that he acted like a man possessed—dancing around furiously, flailing his arms, leaping up, writhing and making ridiculous contortions. The men stood around swaying drunkenly and clapping out a rhythm. In the midst of his wild dance, John's hat flew off and fell overboard.

In the bright moonlight, John could see his hat floating in the sea. "Hey," he yelled drunkenly, "that's my Sunday-go-to-meeting hat. I'm going after it." He staggered to the edge of the ship and poised to leap overboard, thinking he could jump into the small boat alongside.

"Hold it," one of the men shouted, "you drunken fool." And as John lunged forward the sailor caught him by the coat just as he was going overboard.

Lying on his face on the deck John swore loudly, "Whatcha do that for!"

"What are *you* trying to do, drown yourself? That small boat was twenty feet away, and you would have missed it by a long shot. You know you can't swim."

John didn't know how close he had been to disaster. The tide was strong; his friends too drunk to have been able to pull him out of the water, and the rest of the crew was asleep.

Sobered by the thought of John's close call, the men called it a night and went each to his own place to sleep.

John was unaware of it until much later, but this was another act of Providence—the mercy of the God he didn't believe existed.

And that was not the only time his life was spared....

fourteen

Lost in the Jungle

/T HAPPENED while they were at Cape Lopez. John and several others went ashore looking for game. They shot a wild cow, cut it up and took part of it on board. Bending a small tree and securing it with branches, John marked the place where they left the rest of the fresh carcass. Toward evening the men returned for the rest of the cow, lest a wild animal should get it.

"Golly," one of the boys exclaimed, "I can't remember the place."

"Cheer up," John said, confident as usual. "I know just where it is. Follow me."

The men tramped around until it began to get dark. Finally they began deriding John. "All right, smart Alec, you said you knew where it was."

John looked in every direction, trying to find the bent tree. "I was sure it was here...just about here...it has to be in this direction."

But the farther they plunged into the jungle, the more they realized they were lost. When they found themselves waist deep in the swamps, John finally admitted, "Well, boys, it looks like we're lost." By this time it was quite dark. There was no moon, and they had brought neither compass nor weapons, water or food.

With this realization, the jungle sounds became terrifying; they stayed close together, scared out of their skins. No one said it aloud, but they all knew the place was virgin territory, inhabited only by leopards, snakes, poisonous insects. At every crack of a branch, they shook with terror, expecting some ravenous beast to leap at them from behind a bush.

"What shall we do?" the men said among themselves. John, always the spokesman, said, "We'd better keep moving. If only it weren't so bloody dark, we could get an idea of the direction we're going."

After an hour of cautiously tramping around, the clouds began to part and the moon appeared. "Hooray," the men shouted, "here comes our light and it's pointing to the eastern quarter."

"Look at that," a sailor said, "We've even been going in exactly the opposite direction." Giving John a poke in the back, he said, "You told us we were going in the right direction. What we were doing was getting deeper into the jungle. If we had kept this up another hour, we'd have been hopelessly lost. Some guide you are!"

"Just be glad you didn't make lunch for a lion," John retorted.

Actually, the fact that no wild animal approached them, and the fact that the moon began to shine was just one more act of Providence in John's behalf—something which he realized years later. Right now he called it luck.

Neither at this time nor at any time before had it ever occurred to John to give thanks to God. He had no thought at all of God, nor any consciousness of his need for God. Because he had constantly ignored the tuggings of conscience, his conscience seemed to have stopped functioning. It was as though he had sinned against the Holy Spirit and was abandoned even by God Himself.

He was so far from God that even sickness and near scrapes with death had absolutely no effect on him. His philosophy was that death is the end of existence. He would be neither with angels nor with devils because he was convinced they did not exist.

About a year after John had joined the *Greyhound* crew, the captain completed his business. After a brief stop at the island of Anabona for supplies, he gave orders to sail for England. It was early in January, 1748.

As they set sail, John approached the captain. "How long before we are home, sir?"

"Getting homesick?" We're a long way from England, young man. About seven thousand miles—that's because of the circuitous route we have to make in order to take advantage of the trade winds.

John was getting more and more bored. He whiled away some of the time by again studying mathematics from *Euclid*. He strolled on deck, looking for chances to entertain someone with his blasphemous jokes.

As they sailed on, the captain told him they were now near the coast of Brazil, then would stop at Newfoundland to fish for cod. All of that took about six weeks. Finally they headed for home on March first. "We're in luck," said the captain; "this strong wind will push us home in good time."

"Wonderful!" cried John; "I'm getting terribly bored with nothing to do."

The captain looked at John with disturbed eyes. "We'd better get home in a hurry. Twenty months in the tropics has made havoc of the ship. We've already made a lot of repairs; the dried-out timbers have been caulked over and over. The sails and cordage are badly worn. Just hope we don't run into any stormy weather, because this old boat can't take it."

"We'll make it fine," John replied with his usual bravado. "And before long we will be in England celebrating with wine, women, and song."

The captain looked at him wryly. "You can have all of that; I've got a wife to come home to."

"So what difference would that make? You can have the wife and the girls as well."

The captain said nothing, not wanting to get into an argument. Anxiously he watched the sky, troubled at the gathering clouds and the cold winds which sent his off-duty men scurrying below deck to get some warmth to bodies accustomed to the heat of the tropics.

At first John was excited about the homeward trip, but within a week, he became restless again. It was March 9, and as he had done often before he picked up *Thomas à Kempis*. As before, he read it just for diversion, like a newspaper. But this time something different happened.

From whence it came he knew not, but a strangely foreign thought entered his mind: *What if it's true what à Kempis says, all this about the punishment of sin, of going to hell, of God's judgment. What if it is true...*

And for the first time in many years, a glimmer of light shone into the blackness and deadness of his conscience so defiled by willful sin. Disgusted at his feelings—his weakness he called it—he slammed the book shut and tossed it on a table. "So what if this is true, then I'll pay the penalty for my owns sins. And that's that!" And he went up on deck to talk to the fellows.

After engaging in talk about what they would do when they got home—including girls at the taverns and parties—John went to bed. But not before he glanced at the sky somewhat anxiously. It looked very threatening, even in the dark and the wind was rising, the billows were immense.

It was late and he was tired, so the moment he sank into his pillow he was sleeping soundly.

Suddenly, he was awakened by unusual noises. "What is that?" he mumbled as he came out of his sleep. He heard the crash of splintering wood, felt the ship jar and toss violently. Then to his utter amazement, the sea began pouring down from the deck, covering the floor of the cabin with icy water. Shocked, he sprang up, pulled on his clothes. From above he heard shouting, "The boat is sinking! We're going down!"

Sloshing through the rapidly rising water, he started for the ladder to go on deck. He was part way up when the captain shouted from above, "Go back and get a knife, hurry!"

A moment later, as he was returning up the ladder with the knife, to his horror, the man who was on the deck just above the ladder (the exact place where he would have been had he not returned for the knife) was engulfed by a huge wave and washed overboard into the blackness.

No time to try a rescue which would have been futile. John turned to the captain for orders. As he looked around he saw gale winds churning the sea into a huge, heaving mass of billows which tossed the ship violently and washed over the deck repeatedly. The fury of the wind and waves had already savagely torn away timbers on one side and began to wreck other parts of the damaged ship.

The captain rapidly snapped orders. To some he said, "Man the pumps," to others, "Start bailing with buckets." To others, "Get every piece of blanket, clothing, anything, and stuff the leaks. Then nail boards over them. We've got to save the ship."

John joined the men in their desperate efforts but after an hour it looked hopeless. Mountainous waves kept washing over the ship and pouring into the cabins below.

At one time John was near the captain and heard him

say, "If we didn't have the beeswax, and the light wood on board, we would have sunk by now."

The men continued bailing and pumping.

As powerful, angry waves relentlessly washed over the deck, the captain ordered all hands to tie themselves to the nearest immovable object, lest they be swept overboard. After hours of frantically working on leaks and bailing water, John noticed that the waves were getting smaller, the wind less furious. Elated, he shouted, "She's calming down, the storm has abated!" From above and below deck he heard weary shouts of joy.

In the midst of their relief, the men huddled miserably to whatever shelter was near, shaking with cold. Their thin summer clothes soaked with the salty sea were no protection from the elements.

The captain walked from one group to the other. "We're by no means out of danger, just keep the pumps going and keep up the bailing. That wind is beginning to start up again."

During the stress John tried his old tricks of entertaining the men. "Cheer up fellows, in a few days this storm will be over, and we'll be talking about it over our wine. It will be something to write home about."

A sailor looked at him woefully as he kept bailing. "It's too late now; we're done for."

"Don't be so pessimistic," John retorted. "We'll pull through. This isn't the first storm you've been in, chump."

But as he looked over the situation, John realized that it indeed looked hopeless. The storm had begun anew, violent winds tossed the ship as though it were a toy; powerful waves broke over it and poured down into the cabins below. All their efforts to plug up holes, to pump and to bail water seemed futile.

Later in the day, tired from pumping and feeling utterly miserable, John walked on deck toward the captain. After a few words, telling him they were keeping up their efforts, John said almost without thinking...and addressing his words to no one in particular..."If this will not do, the Lord have mercy on us!" It was nine o'clock in the morning. (Later, John distinctly remembered the day and hour.)

The moment he said those words, he was shocked and surprised at himself. This was the first time in years that he had even mentioned the name of God in anything but blasphemy and mockery.

No sooner had he spoken than he realized, "Mercy—what mercy is there for me—the way I have lived and acted..."

Since the captain had ordered him to return to the pump he remained there until noon, lashing himself to a post lest the waves should wash him overboard. As he again felt the ship go down deep, deep to the bottom of a huge billow, he trembled with terror, thinking, "She'll never come up, she'll sink this time." He groaned in despair.

"And if she does, if I drown, then what. Oh my God, then what?" And he alternated between anger and despair and hope. "So what if we survive, God would never forgive me. He isn't that kind of God. But God... am I saying God?... No, there isn't any. Yes there is, there must be. Oh my God...."

fifteen

Shipwreck

From three in the morning until noon, John furiously pumped out water. Finally, he dragged himself into his sea-soaked room and collapsed onto his soggy bunk, mumbling "I don't care if I ever get up. I'm done in!"

Just an hour later he was awakened from a deep sleep by the captain calling, "John, you're on duty again." He staggered up the ladder to the deck and stood limply before the captain. "I am sorry, sir, but I haven't any strength left for pumping." For a moment the captain looked at him then said, "Very well, then, take the helm." Grateful for the change, John remained at the helm until midnight, taking off only a few moments to eat.

While at his solitary task of steering the ship through the heaving sea, he now had time to reflect on his past life. From out of his subconsciousness emerged scriptures his mother had urged him to memorize when he was only seven—scriptures which he thought he had forgotten. Unknown to him, the Holy Spirit was beginning to convict him of sin, righteousness and judgment (John 16:8).

Why did he have to remember that long passage in Proverbs? It poured through his mind like the sea water had poured into his cabin.

"Because I have called, and ye refused; I have stretched out my hand, and no man regarded; But ye have set at nought all my counsel, and would none of my reproof.... Therefore shall they eat of the fruit of their own way and be filled with their own devices" (Proverbs 1:24-31).

Suddenly, a thought struck him like a blow. *If this ship goes down, I will go to hell! Oh how rotten I am, how filthy, how blasphemous and adulterous! I am a great sinner.*

All through the lonely hours of the stormy night, remorse tore at his heart like the winds now tore at the remaining scraps of sails clinging to broken masts.

At noon he was relieved of his duty at the steering wheel and allowed to rest a while before taking his turn at the pump. At last the efforts of the twelve men began to avail. At six in the evening, the captain walked through the ship, talking to his men. "Boys, the ship is finally clear of water."

Almost too exhausted to feel emotion, weak from hunger and shivering from cold, the haggard men could only breathe sighs of relief.

But John did more than that. Now an unfamiliar thought entered his mind. *God is having mercy on us.*

That evening as he lay on his bed, shivering in his ocean-drenched clothing, he thought of the Lord Jesus whose name he had used only in mockery and blasphemy and cursing. *Maybe there is hope for such a wicked man as I. Jesus died for my sins. How can it be?*

And yet, conflicting thoughts also tormented him. For too many years he had trained his mind to discount everything that had to do with faith. *Evidence, scientific proof, that is what is needed. This is the Age of Reason; what proof is there of the deity of Christ, of the authority of the scriptures?*

But those thoughts of the non-existence of God only increased his misery. He was afraid to die. *Oh how I wish I could truly believe; how I wish it were all true, everything that mother taught me; everything the Bible says....*

To compound his internal distress, the next day the captain came to him, his face like a thundercloud. "All this is your fault; this whole thing! My cargo is gone, the ship ruined; we lost one man overboard...I told you we would be punished for the way you carried on. You're a Jonah! I have half a mind to throw you out! Then we will be sure to reach our destination. Right now even with the water bailed out, the ship is in such bad condition, I still doubt if we'll ever make it to land." And he left abruptly.

This time there were no smart retorts from John. He knew that he was a Jonah indeed and that perhaps the captain was right. Perhaps God was punishing him and the whole crew on his account. His misery was acute.

Without knowing how, in a wordless way, John continued sending up thoughts, prayers, pleas—he knew not what. And God did hear those feeble, agonized efforts at prayer for the storm began to abate.

The *Greyhound*, however, was still a good distance from England and by no means out of danger and now far less able to cope. As for food and provisions, most of the livestock had been washed overboard by the violence of the waves, the casks of food had been broken into slivers and those that remained intact were soaked with salty sea water. All that was edible were a few codfish and a little food that had been kept for the hogs.

As the captain ordered the dividing of half a cod among his twelve men he said, "I'm sorry, men, if we don't land soon, we'll starve."

In the past these terrible emotions would have evoked from John volleys of curses and blasphemies. But to his own surprise, he discovered that his tongue had been mysteriously tamed. Not that he made any conscious effort; it just happened. (Later he realized it was the work of the Holy Spirit.)

He was still a long way from a real relationship with God; there were still too many doubts in his mind. But at least he felt ready to investigate, to read the scriptures, to find out if there was evidence enough to dispel the doubts instilled in him by the reading of Lord Shaftesbury's books and strengthened by the atheist he had consorted with on board the HMS *Harwich*.

So, as they continued to limp over the surging sea, John was often in the cabin reading the New Testament— not to mock as formerly, but in a desperate attempt to convince himself that God was real and that the Bible was truly the Word of God and not of man.

As John continued to obey the captain's orders, he noticed that he looked at him with questions in his eyes. John was different, he himself realized that. There were no more foul words coming out of his mouth, no more jokes about God or religion. A number of times the captain walked into the cabin which he still shared with the youth, saw him reading the Bible and looked at him with a warning look. "I know what he is thinking," John said to himself, "that I'm planning some new blasphemies and ridicule of scripture."

At other times the captain cast toward John baleful looks as though to say, "No more of this blasphemy, 'Jonah', we've had enough of God's punishment on account of you."

But John was convinced that God was now having mercy on him and on the ship, for the wind continued to be moderate, the weather was fair and the ship edging painfully toward England.

The main problem now was food. If meagerly rationed they had barely enough to keep them alive for one week. Then it was the condition of the ship with hardly any sails to catch whatever favorable wind blew their way.

After five days of sailing in uncertainty, one of the men suddenly shouted, "Land, we have sighted land!" Everybody rushed on deck. The captain grabbed the binoculars and as his men huddled around him hopefully he said, "It looks like a mountainous coast, perhaps the northwest corner of Ireland. Hurrah boys, let's celebrate. We'll soon reach port!"

Amidst the whoops and joyful hollers of the sailors, the mate remained gloomy. "I'm not sure it is land, captain." As the day advanced, he proved to be only too true. It was a mirage, a cloud formation. Now the whole crew was again plunged into deep disappointment. Added to that, another gale wind arose from the south and continued for two solid weeks of terror.

Everyone knew by the anxious looks on the faces of captain and mate that their troubles had begun again. The men had to continue working hard at the pumps in order to keep the ship afloat. Cold and starving, they were hardly able to keep working. One man died, so weakened by hunger and exposure.

In the midst of despair, hope sprang up as once more the wind shifted to a more favorable position for the disabled ship. Again there were shouts of "Land, land is sighted!" And this time it was no mirage.

It was April 8, just one month since the storm broke. They sighted the island of Tory, and the next day anchored in Lough Swilly, Ireland.

The timeliness of their arrival was shown by the fact that on this day the last of the remaining food was boiling in the pot, as the starving sailors watched with mouths watering.

As soon as the ship anchored, the captain gave orders for the crew to go ashore. Like madmen, they used their remaining strength to leap gleefully out of the ship and dance on the shore. "We're safe, we're safe," they shouted, their gaunt faces alight with relief and joy.

They had been safely anchored for only two hours when the wind again blew up a terrific gale. As the captain stood watching the renewed fury of the waves, he said to John, "Do you see that? If we had remained on the ship just one more night, she would have gone down and all of us with it."

John didn't know whether to tell the captain the words that formed in his heart, "That's because God has answered the prayers of this poor sinner. I know that's why he had mercy on us." But all he said was, "Thank God we are safe on land."

The captain looked at John as though he didn't believe what he was hearing. And later, as John cautiously felt out the rest of the crew, he discovered to his surprise that not one man of them attributed their safety to the mercy of God.

But no matter what the rest thought, John was now convinced that God was real. He could not say that he had fully committed himself to the Lord Jesus. But one thing he knew: he was no longer an infidel. And through his most recent reading of the scriptures, he had become convinced that the Bible was indeed the Word of God.

Not only did he now believe in the existence of God and the authority of the scriptures, but his profanity, blasphemy, cursing were forever gone. He was a changed man.

The crew now clustered around the captain awaiting orders.

"The first thing we need to do is to find food, and the next thing, shelter," he announced. "Let's go and look up yonder."

Weakened by starvation, by the labor of bailing water, by the emotional stress they had undergone, the men now suddenly gained new strength at the words of the captain.

"Food, food, hooray!" they shouted. "We're going to eat again!"

John joined the ragged, drenched company as they clambered over rocks, following the captain into the nearest village. There the Irish received the bedraggled group with great kindness, providing food and clothing and shelter.

sixteen

The Change

FTER THE captain and his men were refreshed, he asked John to accompany him to arrange for the repairs of the disabled ship. When the carpenters examined the vessel they shook their heads. "She's a wreck, Captain. How did you ever survive that bad storm?"

"With my wonderful crew and just pure luck."

"Plus the good hand of God," added John—just as surpised as the captain to hear himself say that.

For a moment the carpenters stared at John, eyebrows raised, then one of them remarked, "The ship sure took a beating. But we'll do our best to make her seaworthy again. It will take a good six weeks."

As the captain and John walked back to the village John asked, "Captain, would you mind if I went to Londonderry while the ship is being repaired?"

"Not at all; go ahead and have a good time. You deserve it."

In Londonderry John rented a room, then explored the little town. When he saw the steeple of a church he thought, *Of course I must attend.* And so he began to go to morning and evening prayers daily. How strange to be inside a church for the first time since childhood! The stained glass windows, the soft light of the candles aroused in him a sense of worship. One day as he talked with the parson, he told him what God had done and asked on what day the sacrament would be given.

With deep emotion, he kneeled on communion day, his hands clasped. "Thank you God for your mercies to me. You saved me from drowning. In my sinful state I would have gone to hell. Thank you for delivering me from the sins of profanity and blasphemy. Most of all, for enlightening my darkened soul." As he partook of the sacred elements, he vowed, "With your help, God, I want to live for you the rest of my life."

During the six weeks it took to repair the ship, John did a lot of thinking—about his past and his future. He now considered himself a believer. He had repented of his sins, and believed that through God's mercy in Christ Jesus he had been forgiven.

And now his thoughts turned again to home. He had learned by talking with people on the island that the *Greyhound* had not been heard of for over eighteen months and was given up as lost. "My father and Mary no doubt think I am at the bottom of the sea. I will have to let them know the truth."

First he wrote to his father.

"Dear Father, I am happy to tell you that I am still alive, though our ship nearly went down. We finally made it and are now in Lough Swilly, Ireland, for repairs. Please do me the favor of finding out whether Mary Catlett is married. If she is still free, I would appreciate your consent and your obtaining that of the Catletts in my behalf."

To John's great delight, he received good news from his father.

"Dear Son, I am very glad to hear you are alive. I thought your ship had surely gone down. I took time off to go to Chatham to visit the Catletts. Mary is not married, and her parents said they would not stop your suit of her. But it is up to Mary to give her consent.

"I am planning to sail to Canada to be governor in Fort York. If you wish, I would be glad to take you along."

John read the letter several times then thought, *Well, well, I see the old gentleman is not as mean as I thought. I feel good about him wanting me to accompany him to Canada, but I couldn't possibly do that.*

The last thing John wanted was to go to Canada. He had been away from his beloved long enough. But he did long to see his father to ask his forgiveness for all the sorrow and inconveniences he had caused him in the past.

Because of the scheduled departure of his ship, Captain Newton was unable to await word from his son, so he sailed without it. John arrived in Liverpool at the end of May, 1748, just a day after his father had left. Greatly disappointed, John wrote a long letter and sent it on the next outgoing ship.

Now as he stood on the shore watching the ship sail into the horizon, the old worries began to torment him. "Here I am expecting to ask a girl to marry me and I don't even have a job."

Hands in pockets, John paced the shore, pondering. "Should I forget my pride and appeal to Joseph Manesty? What if he turns me down? Then I'll have to delay my trip to Chatham and try to find work elsewhere. But with my reputation, who would want me?" His longing to see Mary overcame all his fears and soon he was in Manesty's office.

"Why hello, John," he said, "what brings you here? I heard about the ship's mishap and its good fortune in surviving. The captain had some good words to say about you."

John brightened. "Oh he did!... As the captain probably told you, I am not the same person as when I was first on the *Greyhound*."

John proceeded with his pleas, desperate now because of his determination to win Mary. "Please, sir, would you be willing to give me a job on one of your ships? I am twenty-three years old and am experienced as a naval and merchant sailor. I assure you, I have learned my lessons about conduct and promise to be responsible and dependable."

Mr. Manesty scrutinized Newton. "Yes, I agree. I understand that you proved yourself during the storm. I also hear you have had a great moral change, which I must say is very commendable.

"I will tell you what I will do. I am outfitting the *Brownlow* to sail to Africa for slaves. Suppose I make you captain? Do you think you could handle that?"

Captain! Did John hear him right? Captain?

John at first beamed his pleasure at the offer, then his face clouded. "I appreciate your confidence in me, sir, but I believe I had better start in a subordinate position. I need to learn how to obey and take heavy responsibilities."

Looking pleased, Mr. Manesty replied, "All right, that's a good suggestion. I will sign you on as mate. And after you have proved yourself, you can later take the captaincy of another ship."

"Thank you, sir, thank you very much," said John and the two men shook hands.

With his means of livelihood now assured, John proceeded with the plans nearest to his heart—to get Mary to promise to marry him. According to his father's report, the Catletts had already consented. But Mary had not yet committed herself. Was it because she wasn't sure she cared enough for him?

In less than a week, John was knocking at the gate of the Catlett home. Again, as at the first visit, the dog barked, the chickens squawed, and the cat fled in alarm; and out of the front door came bursting the entire family.

What a welcome he received! "John, how good to see you after so long. My, but you look prosperous! Do come in." As always, Mrs. Catlett dominated the scene.

John had difficulty restraining himself enough to politely greet the family, but he had eyes only for Mary. How charming she looked! The lovely bud had blossomed into a full-blown rose, far more beautiful than the first time he had seen her and had fallen in love with her.

"Mary," he almost whispered her name as he greeted her. "Mary." He looked at her with eyes and face alight with love and admiration. How he longed to be alone with her, but he had to meet first with the family in the familiar dining room, drink tea, and tell of his adventures (which he abbreviated in order to get it over with).

During his narrative, John touched upon the change God had brought into his life. He sensed that they seemed uncomfortable with his story of a spiritual change, so he did not elaborate.

To make a favorable impression, John also informed them that he was to be mate on the *Brownlow* and was promised the captaincy the following year.

After his story was told, John indicated that he wished to speak to the Catletts and Mary alone, so Mrs. Catlett dispersed the other children. John cleared his throat. "My father told me that you have no objection to my interest in your daughter."

"Yes, that is what we said and we still mean it," said

Mrs. Catlett, as spokesman. Mr. Catlett simply nodded. "But of course, Mary has the final say."

There was an awkward silence as John and Mary looked at each other, embarrassed and shy.

"Well Mother," said Mr. Catlett, "I guess we will have to let the young people be alone for awhile to talk things over." And so saying, he led his wife into the kitchen.

Still embarrassed and not knowing how to proceed, John said, "Mary, let's go outside where we can talk more freely." His heart beat wildly as he took her by the arm and led her out the front door. The moment they were outside, Mary pulled herself away, not harshly, but rather through modesty.

For awhile they walked in silence, John struggling to mouth the words which brimmed in his heart: "Mary," he wanted to say, "I love you deeply. Do you, can you...care fore me...will you promise me..." But the words stuck in his throat. To his utter dismay, he was so tongue-tied that he couldn't get the words out.

Surely she can read my thoughts, he said to himself, *and see the love in my eyes, the anguish in my soul, my inability to express myself! Why can't she understand? Is there a hint of amusement in her eyes as she watches me struggle? Why doesn't she help me out and make it easy for me. Surely she must know what I long to say!*

But she simply looked down, self-possessed, poised, and silent. Finally, she said, "It's getting dark. We'd better go into the house."

Deeply disappointed, John later went to the upstairs

room chiding himself for his stupid silence. "Why, that's the whole reason I came—to ask her to marry me. Now I muffed it. What an idiot I am!"

It was nearly morning before he finally fell asleep.

Early the next day, John had to leave without anything definite from Mary. Since there was still some time before the *Brownlow* would sail from Liverpool, he stopped at the home of his stepmother in London and wrote Mary a long letter. As always, he was able to express himself better in writing than in speaking.

> *"Dear Mary, As I told you, I will be gone for about a year. You know that I have loved you since the day I saw you, but you have never let me know how you feel about me. I believe you are fond of me, but I still do not know whether you love me. I am not even now asking you to declare what you don't feel. But please promise that you will at least write while I am at sea. And, dare I ask you not to consider anyone else until I have returned? Please, Mary, I beg you. John."*

Since he was short of funds for fare and inns, he decided to walk the 300 kilometers back to Liverpool, which took three days. During that time he thought much of his spiritual change and of his hopes of getting Mary. When he finally reached his destination, tired and dusty with his fine clothes wrinkled, he found lodging and eagerly awaited Mary's reply. It came much sooner than he had expected.

> *"Dear John, It was good to hear from you. Yes, I am fond of you but cannot say I am in love. Although, I must say you are quite a different person than the one you were when I first met you. In fact, you have become so religious that you almost seem too good for me. And yet, I like the change. You are more cheerful and not so gloomy and moody as you used to be. Yes, I will promise to write and also that I will not commit myself to anyone else until you return from your trip. But I am not saying that I am making any definite promise as to our relationship. Mary."*

seventeen

Total Surrender

AVING THAT promise from Mary, he sighed with relief. Now he could give serious attention to his work as mate on the *Brownlow*, collecting a cargo of slaves from Guinea.

The first night on the seas, John stood on the deck gazing into the majestic star-studded canopy above and listening to the rhythmic slapping of waves against the sides of the ship. His heart lifted in worship to the Maker of this awesome immensity. How great God is! How good, how kind that He should have had mercy on such a sinner as he had been! It was amazing grace.

Yet, as his heart swelled with gratitude, he was vaguely conscious that whatever meager relationship he had established with God had somehow weakened recently.

No longer did he agonize about Mary, for he felt secure in her promise to write and to wait for him. Nor did he have to worry about his future, for he had a good job and promise of a better one. For some reason he no longer read the Bible as eagerly as he had when he first began his quest during and after the storm at sea.

With these troubling thoughts about his spiritual state, John went down to his cabin.

As they continued to sail toward Guinea, with time on his hands, John joined the other sailors, joking about taverns, women, and good times and unconsciously inflaming the lust which lay not too deeply buried in his heart. Small wonder then that when they went inland he was unable to resist the enticements of the women who frequented the taverns. Three drinks of rum and he found himself eagerly following a scantily clad brunette into a side room.

At every inland stop, he was overtaken by his besetting sin. One morning after a night of carousing, he lay in his bunk with a miserable hangover—his stomach queasy, his head bursting with pain. As he stared into space, conviction gripped him. "Oh my God, what has happened to me? I'm worse than I was before. How could this happen, how could it? After the great mercy God has shown me."

But each time the hangover wore off, the conviction faded and his physical demands overrode the increasingly faint tuggings of conscience and of the Holy Spirit.

In regard to his consorting with the female negro slaves, John was following a practice common among seamen. So he found it easy to rationalize his own conduct—they were all doing it—officers and crew alike.

After days of sailing—his lusts indulged by night, his

duties performed by day—John became bored and restless. One day, with the *Brownlow* anchored in Sierra Leone, he decided to stop at the Plantanes to visit Claw and Williams. (Unconsciously he was seeking diversion to dispel his growing feeling of guilt.)

As he sailed further inland in the longboat, he saw familiar landmarks—small inlets, clumps of trees, islands—and then came into full view of the compound where Claw and his servants lived.

Memories of his former captivity flooded his mind: The misery of his terrible attack of jungle fever, the awful treatment he had received from jealous, vindictive PI, the cruel and harsh conduct and false accusations of Claw, the overwhelming loneliness, and the humiliation of being ministered to and, even once, ridiculed by PI's slaves.

With growing excitement, he anchored his boat and strode toward the compound, eager for Claw to see the change in his appearance and to inform him of the turn in his fortunes.

Near the house he observed a small grove of young lime trees, the ones he had planted when he was there. It was here that Claw had made the sarcastic prediction: "Who knows, by the time these trees bear fruit, you could return from England as captain of your own ship." How strange that Claw should have made such a prediction, which would soon come to pass!

As he was musing, he observed a couple approaching from the far end of the grove. Yes, it was Claw and PI—

PI stouter and more gaudily dressed than ever; and Claw, having acquired a paunch, doubtless from PI's rich and abundant meals. How well John remembered that neither Claw nor PI ever made the slightest attempt to regulate their "healthy" appetites!

The two stared at John then hurried toward him hands extended. "Well, blow me down," exclaimed Claw, "if it ain't John Newton hisself! What a surprise and what a pleasure!"

PI looked him over from head to foot, admiration in her eyes. "My, but you do look handsome and so prosperous. What brings you here?"

In her characteristic fashion, after they began conversing, she laughed loudly and heartily, and Claw went to slapping John on the back, spouting lusty jokes and raw humor.

Later, while they enjoyed cool drinks on the veranda, John told them all that had happened since they parted, including his near shipwreck and of the offer by Mr. Manesty to be mate on this trip and on the next, captain.

Then John pointed to the grove of lime trees. "Remember, Claw, your predication that I would be back from Englandwith my own ship by the time there were limes on those trees? Well, sir, it will happen next year."

John felt a deep satisfaction in informing the pair of the reversal of his fortunes. All that Claw could say was, "That is something, ain't it?"

Late in the afternoon, John headed toward the other end of the island to visit his friend Williams. While making his way over the rough terrain, his heart warmed at the remembrance of his good treatment by this man. And when they now met, they had a great time of renewing their friendship. Williams begged Newton to stay a while.

The next day, while Williams was away on business, to John's dismay he felt himself getting sick and sicker. *Oh, no,* he thought, *am I getting jungle fever again? I hate to have this happen here.*

However, he need not have worried, for after Williams learned of his guest's illness, he was very considerate. "I am sorry," John began to say, "I don't want to impose..."

"Think nothing of it," Williams broke in; "it could happen to anyone. I'm just glad it happened here where my servants can take care of you."

As John lay in bed, so weak and ill that he wondered if he would even survive, he began to review his recent lapses into his old sinful ways. "How could I?" he lamented. "After all that God has done for me."

Although the fever raged, his head was bursting with throbbing pain, and he was so weak he was hardly able to even sit up, he knew he must get alone with God. For his spiritual misery far outweighed his physical pain.

With great effort he struggled out of bed and, by holding on to a chair, managed to stand on wobbly legs. The servant looked at him in alarm and begged him to lie down. But John insisted, "I must go somewhere and be alone, I must." Thinking John was delirious, the servant kept imploring him not to go, but John insisted. The servant stood on the veranda, hands clasped tightly, anxiously watching the sick man.

John staggered up the beach for about a mile until he found the same cavelike shelter where he had resorted for comfort while working for Claw. Sinking down beneath the overhanging rock, he breathed hard, recovering from his strenuous walk.

When his panting subsided, he fell flat on his face. "Oh, God, forgive me; I'm sorry. I don't know why I carried on the way I did. I don't know if I ever really made a full surrender to you. I don't think I did. I must have been relying on myself to make it. I don't know; I don't know.

"But now, Oh God, I surrender myself wholly to you, wholly, wholly. Please accept me."

As his tears mingled with the sandy beach, it was as though a great weight of sin had lifted, and he felt an inner peace far deeper and stronger than any he had ever experienced before.

Years later, when speaking of his experience at this time, he wrote, "I never again returned to the black declensions of my youth."

When he finally arose, he was amazed to find himself stronger in body and buoyant in soul. Although still weak, he was able to walk to the Williams house without too much difficulty. There he saw the servant still standing on the veranda, but now his anxiety turned into amazement. "Mr. Newton, you look better, much better. How glad Mr. Williams will be!"

Two days later John was able to return to his longboat and sail it back to the ship. On board the *Brownlow*, he once more began to read the Bible and to pray, not because he had to but because he wanted to.

For eight months they ranged the coast, stopping at various locations for slaves. On his trips ashore in the longboat he encountered many dangers—hours of exposure to the burning sun in the day, chilling dews and heavy rains at night, snakes and wild animals in the jungles; bad-tempered or treacherous natives (several white men had been poisoned or killed).

Among his own crew, he helped bury seven who died from jungle fever. Several times his own boat had been overturned by heavy surf or waves, and he was dragged to land as dead, for he could not swim. Not the least of the hazards were the old temptations with women, but now, by the help of God, he could resist.

Each night as John returned from an inland trip, he thanked God for His watchful care over His most unworthy servant. Bible reading and prayer became as natural to him as eating, for he felt nourished in his soul.

As they prepared to go to the West Indies, the captain ordered John to take some men with him and go down Rio Castors for wood and water to bring aboard. With a cheerful "Aye, aye, sir," he was almost in the boat ready to let go of the ropes, when the captain leaned over the side of the ship and called, "Hey John, come back on board." Surprised, he clambered back up expecting that the captain had forgotten some further instructions. "Yes, sir, is there anything more?"

"No," replied the captain, "I just decided you should

remain on board today," and he sent another man in John's place.

Puzzled, John asked, "Any particular reason?"

"No, I just want you to stay here today." Never before had that longboat gone in for supplies without him, but John obeyed the order, and the boat went without him.

In the morning they waited longer than usual for the return of the boat. Finally they were surprised to see another boat pull alongside the *Brownlow.*

"I have bad news for you, sir," the stranger said to the captain. "Last night your longboat sank and all your men drowned in the river. I'm afraid the sharks got their corpses."

Shocked, the captain and John looked at each other. For hours neither of the two said what was in his mind, for they were too stunned by the tragedy. Later in the afternoon John said, "Captain, I would have been dead, except that you ordered me not to go. It must be nothing else but the mercy of God which spared my life."

The captain shook his head in wonder. "It must be. I had no reason at all to detain you. The good Lord must have some plans for you."

When their business was finished, they set sail for England and, after an absence of over a year, arrived back in Liverpool.

"John," said the captain, "you have done a fine job. I am sure Mr. Manesty will give you the captaincy of a ship on the next trip."

"Thank you for your good words," John replied. Now,

eager to wind up business matters pertaining to the trip, he hurried to a stationary shop, bought supplies, and wrote to Mary, asking her to marry him.

Day after day he anxiously awaited her reply. When it came, he was greatly disappointed, for she turned him down. Twice more he wrote, pleading, but twice again she refused him, giving various reasons.

John was deeply hurt. He had thought all obstacles were removed: his character was changed for the better; he had the promise of a good job; his father and her parents had consented. Now Mary herself became the obstacle to his happiness.

"Oh God, oh God," he prayed. "You know how tongue-tied I get in her presence. What must I do? Please tell me." After he prayed in deep distress he decided to return to Chatham and try again in person to persuade her to change her mind.

eighteen

The Duke of Argyle

ONCE AGAIN he rented a horse for his trip. The closer he came to Chatham, the harder he prayed. As in so many times past, he now stood before the door, his heart beating with anticipation. To his delight, Mary herself opened the door.

"Mary," he said, "Mary, you are so lovely. Mary..." And he didn't know what else to say. But surely his eyes, full of love, must be saying it. Yet as he looked into her eyes, he saw no response, only calm neutrality. "Come, let's go out and walk." Without mentioning the cold, Mary put on her coat and scarf and walked with him down the familiar path past the woods.

At first his heart beat so wildly he couldn't speak, but finally he found words. "Mary, you know that I love you and want you to marry me...."

To his surprise, Mary changed from her usual joyful and teasing manner and said firmly, "I can't marry you. Don't mention the matter to me again."

Stunned, but too desperate to be put off, he tried again. But Mary interrupted, "Please don't talk about that." (Did John imagine that her voice was less rigid?)

"But why, Mary, am I so terrible that you can't love me? Is there anything wrong with me?"

"On the contrary," Mary replied, "you are quite different than you used to be. But you have become so religious, I'm afraid you are too good for me. I just couldn't live up to it."

"That's not true, Mary. You are far beyond me in goodness and social graces...and just everything. I'm not worthy of you. But I promise with all my heart that if you marry me, I will spend the rest of my life making you happy."

Mary looked up at him as though she were being slightly convinced. Then her face clouded. "But why should I get married? I'm happy now with my family and friends."

"Don't let a little thing like that worry you," John pleaded. "We will visit your family and friends often. Please, Mary..."

"But, but..." she demurred.

It was getting colder, so they had to return to the house. For several days John kept up his pleas. When he felt he couldn't stay longer, he asked her for a final walk.

Near a turn in the road he stopped, took her by the shoulders, and looked into her eyes. "Mary, look at me. Don't you care for me—just a little?"

"Don't," she said and pulled away. Her back turned,

she was silent for what seemed like a long time. Then suddenly, unexpectedly, she turned toward him, looked up into his face, and literally gave him her hand. "Yes, John," she said.

Unbelieving, John stared at her. "Mary, you don't mean that. I mean...Oh Mary, I..." He was almost beside himself with joy. He wanted to leap and run and shout. Then he tenderly drew her toward him in their first embrace.

"Oh Mary, how I love you. Thank God. Thank God." And when he released her and looked into her eyes, he saw the response. It was love. Her eyes glowed with love. For a while they looked at each other. Then tears welled in Mary's eyes and trickled down her cheeks. "I love you, John," she said. "I've always loved you."

Two weeks later on February 1, 1750, they were married in a simple ceremony in St. Mary's church. He was nearly 25 and she 21. For the first three blissful months, they lived with the Catletts, enjoying the simple pleasures of her day—visits to neighbors and friends, parlor games, plays. This was the kind of thing Mary enjoyed.

But John was different from most of his contemporaries, for he was a great lover of nature. So when spring came, he introduced his bride to the world of trees and flowers, birds and woodland animals. As it turned warmer, they took daily walks in the countryside, delighting in the early signs of spring, kneeling in the damp woods to look for the first anemones, and thrilling at the songs of birds.

In the midst of their happiness a troubling thought began to plague John. He was running out of money and too embarrassed to tell Mary. So he put aside his conscience and did what everyone else was doing—even the church itself—and that was buying lottery tickets. But the more he tried to win the more he lost until he was 70 pounds in debt.

And then, providentially again, he received a letter from Joseph Manesty. Mary stood by him when he opened the letter. "What is it, John...you look so troubled."

"It's from Mr. Manesty; he says my ship *The Duke of Argyle* is ready, and I must go to Liverpool at once."

"Oh, so soon? We've just been married and are so happy."

"Mary, I didn't have the heart to tell you before, but I am out of money and will have to go to work right away." He held her closely. "It will be bitter as death for me to leave you, but I must."

After tearful farewells, they parted. Because his funds were so low that he couldn't afford to pay for coach or horse or inns, he walked back to Liverpool. During his solitary trudging, mile after mile, his former confidence vanished and he was filled with misgivings. "I don't know if I can handle the job of captain...Of course I had experience as mate...But this is different...Of course, I now have the Lord to help me..."

After he finally arrived in Liverpool, he had a conference with Mr. Manesty and learned he would be in charge of a company of thirty—including three mates, a carpenter, and a doctor. The sailing date was scheduled for August 14, 1750.

Manesty and John examined the ship and talked business regarding slaves. Below deck was a large room for the slaves with three compartments, one each of men, women, and children. There were shelves for slaves to lie on rows one above the other, tightly packed like books on a shelf. The men were shackled two by two. The carpenter also built a barricade as protection against insurrection (which danger was always present, as they learned from experience).

There was good reason for a doctor to be present—not only for the sailors but also to keep their cargo of slaves alive and in good health until they reached their destination. Of the 60,000 slaves transported each year in English ships nearly 20,000 died from fever, dysentery, and other illnesses.

It was a grim trade, yet the English felt that when the slaves were bought by "Christian" white people, their lot was greatly improved. And John shared the same philosophy. Nevertheless, he took his responsibility as captain so seriously that he often fasted and prayed for not only his crew but for the slaves as well.

While on his journey toward Africa he wrote Mary almost daily, sending his letters on the nearest ship returning to England. But he had more to do than dream about his bride and write to her. He was captain and had business to attend to.

When they reached the west coast of Africa, he immediately arranged for the purchase of the best slaves at the lowest possible prices, so that when they were sold they would bring a profit for Mr. Manesty.

As John was supervising the placement of the slaves in the ship, he could not help but notice the more attractive females. It disturbed him that his passions were stirred. That night he prayed earnestly for God's help and planned some practical aids.

To help him control what he termed "improper" emotion, he drank only water, often abstained from meat, and at night walked the deck praying for strength and for his beloved Mary. How he missed her! During his leisure moments, all his thoughts were of her, remembering the way she looked, the shine of her hair, the glow of her skin, the light of love in her blue eyes.

Finally, he got two letters from her (which had been transferred from ship to ship seven times before they reached him). He kissed them and read them over and over. One letter brought him sorrow.

> *"I am sorry to tell you that we received word that while your father was swimming, he accidentally drowned."*

Oh how sorry John was that before his father left for Canada, he had not been able to ask his pardon. Yet he was comforted that he had written his father a number of times, asking forgiveness; and that his father had replied kindly and they were beautifully reconciled.

As captain, John conducted a brief service every Lord's day for his thirty men, reading scripture and giving a little talk.

When several ships were anchored nearby, the captains and officers met in each other's ships for fellowship. But when John noticed how they drank and their profanity and worldliness, he felt out of place. He did not care to appear as "holier than thou," yet more than once he excused himself and left early. When the men talked about their experiences with the female slaves John said, "I don't do things like that anymore. Besides, I am now married."

"So, what difference does that make?" one of the captains asked. "I don't think you have the right notion of life."

Newton looked at him calmly. "I am sure *you* haven't."

Another captain jeered, "You are the slave of one woman."

Newton replied, "But you are the slave of many."

When asked the reason for his "piety," John briefly explained what had happened as a result of the near shipwreck.

"Oh, so you got religious because you were afraid to die," one of the men scoffed.

"Yes, that's right. I was afraid to die. In my sinful state, I would have gone straight to hell."

"Hell! That's a good one. We have our hell right here on earth."

"Perhaps you do," replied John, "But I am no longer

having a hell but am closer to having a heaven on earth."

The trip continued without unusual events and on October 7, 1751, he returned to Liverpool. Unfortunately, because of losing men through sickness and accidents, only sixteen of the thirty arrived with him. This was a common hazard of sailing in those days, and so Mary's fears for the safety of her husband were justified.

How thrilled she was to learn that God had taken care of her beloved and had brought him safely back into her arms!

This time John had enough money so he could remain with Mary for eight months of bliss, walking through the woods and countryside, holding hands, and enjoying each other to the fullest.

nineteen

*A*GAIN HE received a letter from Joseph Manesty:

"John, I would like you to make a second journey to collect slaves, this time on the African.

So he sailed in July, 1752. As before he held worship services on his ship, and as before he wrote Mary frequently and prayed for her.

It would seem that a seafaring life away from the influence of Christians and from church would hinder spiritual growth, and yet John found that the benefits compensated for the disadvantages. For whatever inclination he had toward contemplation was greatly enhanced by his solitary evening walks on the deck or when steering the ship. He was alone, alone with himself and alone with God.

During the day he was busy with various duties and in between inland trips there were just the long days of sailing toward their next destination. To pass his time profitably and to prevent boredom, John divided his day into three parts: eight hours for sleep and eating, eight hours for exercise and devotions, and eight hours for studying Latin and good books to improve his mind.

When inland he loved to wander alone through the fantastically beautiful tropical forests near shore. It was during these times that he experienced some of the sweetest times of fellowship with God.

But his life was not all peaceful. One day on board ship John overheard whispering among some of the crew, saw furtive looks, and heard some of the men suddenly stop talking as he approached.

Something wrong is going on here, he thought. Disturbed, he made this a matter of prayer and God answered. Two of the men suddenly became very ill and when one of them died, the survivor, taken with the fear of God, confessed to John. The crew had been plotting to pirate the ship, with these two men being the leaders. Immediately John confronted his second mate. "Are you in on this too?"

"In on what, sir?" the man asked.

"The plot to take over the ship, the piracy..."

"Oh no, sir, I can't believe it! Tell me what happened."

The second mate was so genuinely surprised that John knew he was innocent. With the second mate, and others he found to be with him, John put down the plot and placed the chief offenders in irons for awhile.

(Years later, when he wrote the song "Amazing Grace"

and the verse, "Through many dangers, toils, and snares I have already come," he was speaking not only of his previous trials but of this danger as well.)

But the danger of piracy from his own crew was not all he had to endure. As he was supervising the care of the slaves one afternoon he caught a number of male slaves— huge, muscular men—making suspicious gestures amongst themselves and suddenly stopping when he appeared. Once when John whirled around he saw in the eyes of these same men a guilty expression.

That night as Newton talked to his mate and told of his fears, he asked, "What do you think they're up to?"

"Captain, I am afraid they are also plotting to kill us and seize the ship.... You have been too lenient with them, sir; you have not shackled them securely enough."

John pondered awhile. "I hate to do it; I feel so sorry for them. But I'm afraid that now I will have to...Try to find out the ringleaders and put them in a place by themselves. Put double shackles on their hands and feet...but don't be too rough about it."

"Yes, sir," replied the mate, "but if you don't mind my saying so, these men are cruel savages; they don't have any regard for you or any of us. If they could, they would slit your throat and murder the rest of us. You can't treat them like human beings. They're beasts."

"Perhaps," replied Newton, "but on the other hand, some of my own crew, who are supposedly civilized white men would also do the same if they could."

As they left the west coast of Africa and sailed toward the

West Indies, John was eager to reach the port at St. Christopher's Island for he had asked Mary to address all of her letters there. As soon as the ship was anchored, he made for the makeshift post office. "I'm Captain Newton of the *African*," he said, "and I'm expecting letters from my wife."

"Yes, sir, I will look," replied the man acting as postal agent, speaking English so poorly that John could hardly understand him. Smiling with anticipation, John watched the man go through a box of mail. After a long wait, John became anxious. "I don't see anything addressed to you, sir," the man finally replied.

"It can't be. My wife is very punctual. She always writes. Look again, you must have missed them."

The man searched again, tossing each letter into another box while John carefully looked on. "Sorry, sir, there is nothing for you."

John left the building with a heavy heart. "This isn't like Mary. She must be sick; maybe she died. Something is terribly wrong." And his imagination went into high gear. "Oh God, don't let it be that, please God." He returned to his ship, not only sick at heart but sick in body.

For three weeks he could hardly eat or sleep. Life seemed worthless and he transacted his business like someone in a trance. As he prayed, it finally occurred to him that the letters might have mistakenly been sent to the nearby island of Antigua which was also a port.

At once, he sent a small boat to the island to check it out. To his great relief, there was a packet for him. Of course, his "sickness" suddenly disappeared.

In August, 1753, he returned to Liverpool and from there went on to Chatham. How thrilled he was to tell Mary of his adventures! He said nothing about the attempts of both his crew and the slaves to pirate the ship. Why give her needless worry, since she was never too comfortable about his being on the sea? He did tell her of his scare regarding the letters and they had a good laugh about it.

Then he broke the bad news to her. "Mary, the captain tells me I've got to go again. He has another trip scheduled on the *African* in six weeks."

"Oh John, not again, so soon. It's just too hard to have you away so often. I'm so lonely without you."

twenty

*B*UT HE and Mary had to part and he returned to Liverpool to prepare, wishing he had chosen a better way to make a living. While making arrangements and selecting his crew, he ran into an old friend at the quaysie—Job Lewis, who had been a midshipman with him on the HMS *Harwich*.

"If it isn't my old friend, Job!" exclaimed John.

And Job replied the same way, adding, "What are you up to now? Haven't seen you for years. Let's go over to the tavern and talk things over."

"Not there, let's just talk here," John said. As they conversed, painful memories flooded John's mind. At the time he and Job were friends on the HMS *Harwich*, John had been a deep-dyed athiest, blasphemous, sensual, and had done all he could to win over Job to his philosophy of life. Unfortunately, he had been successful.

Now as they talked, John realized that his friend was still

an athiest. To try to undo the damage John told of the change which had come when he met the Lord and tried in every way to convice him. But it was in vain. Job's reply was, "You were the one who conviced me that this was the Age of Reason and this was the way for intelligent people to live."

"I'm sorry, please forgive me, Job. But I have changed and so can you."

"But I don't want to change. I enjoy being just the way I am."

Sighing, John asked, "What are your plans for the future?"

"Been thinking of going on a ship to Guinea for slaves, but the company I work for went bankrupt. So right now I'm out of a job."

At once, an idea flooded John's mind. "Why not come along with me and be my companion?" he asked. (What he really had in mind was that he might continue his efforts to convert his friend.)

It was not too long before John realized that his efforts were futile. Job was a drunkard, licentious, and profane, mocking God and religion and influencing the other sailors.

As John observed this he said to himself, *My God, this is exactly the way I was before I met You.* The present contrast between his life and that of Job brought him great joy and, yet, great sorrow. Joy because he was no longer a wicked sinner, sorrow because it was through him that his friend had turned against God.

Job proved such a problem and bad influence that

Newton finally bought a small boat, gave him some of his own cargo and put him in charge. He later heard the sad story from others.

One day while inland, Job Lewis had contracted jungle fever and died, crying that he knew he was going to hell but refusing to ask for God's mercy. It was a sad ending to a chapter in John's life. But now a new one was about to begin.

During the six years that he had been following the Lord, John had received very little spiritual help. He read the Bible, prayed, studied devotional books, and attended the services of the Established Church whenever he could. But he never had met anyone who had the evangelical view of spiritual matters. Now it was time for him to receive the help he needed and longed for.

While anchored at St. Christopher's Island and mingling with various captains and officers, he met an Englishman from London, Captain Alexander Clunie. They had not conversed long before John discovered that this man was a true Christian. During the month they remained on the island, they met on each other's ship nearly every night and talked of the things of God.

God used Captain Clunie to explain the difference between the Established Church and the Dissenters. He explained that the latter group proclaimed the necessity of a relationship with Jesus as Savior and Lord and thus reaffirmed John's own experience.

One thing Captain Clunie insisted on was, "John, you must learn to witness more openly concerning your experience with God. It will help you grow in grace."

"But I am reserved by nature," John demurred. "I find it hard to talk to people about this matter; it seems too personal and intimate to relate."

"That's because you have been so accustomed to the formality of the Established Church. I will give you the names and addresses of dissenting churches and people you can contact when you return to England."

"Wonderful! That's what I have been needing all this time."

On August 17, 1754, he returned to England, safe from his third trip.

He returned to Chatham and again spent delightful months with his beloved. He felt so secure and happy in Mary's love that it was like returning to shelter after being in a storm.

But it takes more than love to keep a marriage going and again he needed money to support himself and his wife. With great regret, in the early part of November, 1754, he said, "Mary, I will have to go out again. Oh how I hate to part from you!"

Secretly, he felt a growing distaste for the slave business, so he began to pray, "God, please find me some other employment." And God answered his prayers in an unexpected way.

In the manner that God has of so often coming to our rescue at what we think is the last minute: just two days before sailing time, John and Mary were sitting in the parlor drinking tea and enjoying each other's company. Without warning, John slumped, fell off his chair and lay on the floor like a dead man. For over an hour he remained in a coma, just barely breathing.

Mary fell on her knees beside him crying, "John, what is the matter? Please talk to me. Oh John..." She applied cold cloths to his face, praying and crying to God to help. Her anguish was great. Finally as she watched him intently she saw his eyes open. When he was able to focus, he looked into the face of Mary bending over him. "What happened? Why am I lying here on the floor?"

Almost beside herself with joy, Mary helped him to a chair. "Oh John, I'm so glad you are all right. I was so afraid...How are you? How do you feel? Oh John, I'm so happy...."

Slowly John arose and lay on the couch. "I'm dizzy and my head aches. I don't know what was the matter. Maybe just overly tired. Never mind. It is nothing. It will pass."

The next day he saw a physician and desribed the event of the night before. The doctor advised, "John, I don't know that you should go on a sea trip just now."

After John felt better, he went to Liverpool, explained his condition to Mr. Manesty and resigned command of the ship.

Here again he saw the hand of God which was so evident during all of his life, from childhood and even before he had met the Lord. Mr. Manesty later learned that the ship on which John was to be captain had been taken over by slaves, run ashore, and the captain, second mate, and the doctor murdered.

When John heard this he cried, "Oh my God, I thank

you for your mercy to me again. How often you have proved that your hand is upon me in a most blessed way. Surely you have some good purpose for my life and future."

Everything seemed to be going well, when John began to be disturbed about his wife. "Mary, there's something wrong with you. You're pale and listless. You're just not yourself."

"I know, John. I'm sort of half sick all the time."

The doctor diagnosed her problem as a nervous reaction to John's illness. Despite medication, she steadily became more ill.

Sometimes as they sat together in the parlor, Mary fell asleep in the armchair. John would look at her face, trying not to let himself think, "This is how she will look when she is...oh no, no, God, don't let her die. Please, God. I can't live without her!"

He tried to be cheerful and optimistic in her presence but for nearly a year his unspoken anguish tore at his heart. "Why doesn't God answer my prayer? Why can't the physician do something? Why God, why?" And then he would chide himself for questioning God and would struggle to surrender her to the Lord, for good or for ill.

It was a hard battle. He wanted to remain at her side day and night, but Mary urged, "John, you must go about your duties. I don't like to see you tied down to me like this."

twenty-one

Tide Surveyor
Liverpool

S O, AT her insistence, during more of the following year, John divided his time between London and Chatham. Now thirty years old and with a wife to support, he prayed much about a job. Meanwhile, he looked up the persons and churches in London that his friend Captain Clunie had recommended.

John was pleased with what he saw and heard. These were his first contacts with evangelicals, and he was soon able to relate to them. As he listened to various men of God, he felt like someone who had been wandering in the desert suddenly coming upon an oasis. This is what his soul had been thirsting after, for here was a veritable fountainhead of spiritual nourishment.

But he could not remain in London too long for he had to and wanted to return to Chatham to be with his ailing wife. After remaining with her a while, he returned to London, like a starving man returns to a well-spread table.

Captain Clunie continued to encourage his young protégé to openly witness as to what the Lord had done for him. But John insisted, "I am a great letter writer and in this way do much witnessing. But to do so vocally and personally, I find very difficult. I am still plagued by an inability to express myself. But, God helping me, I will try to do as you suggest."

He began to open up in small testimony meetings which he had started to attend. As he became acquainted with the people, he found it easier to add his testimony to those of others. During the early period of his rapid spiritual growth, John wrote down six resolves:

1. Never again to return to the brutish lusts which once so deeply and so long enslaved me.
2. To get seven hours of sleep.
3. To have one hour of prayer and Bible reading before breakfast.
4. To improve my Latin, French, and mathematics.
5. To avoid unnecessary arguments over trifles.
6. Never to speak ill of others by publishing or repeating their faults.

Despite his happiness in his new contacts and his resolutions for spiritual growth, there remained with him the deep sorrow of the continued illness of his wife. She became so ill that she could hardly bear the sound of footsteps on the carpet in her bedroom. Secretly, John feared her days were numbered.

On top of this worry was his growing concern over

finances, for his supply continued to quickly dwindle because of his wife's medical bills. But God would not let His child become overwhelmed.

One day Mr. Manesty visited John and said, "How would it be if I got you a job as Tide Surveyor in Liverpool? This is a customs service job in which you would have to check incoming and outgoing ships for contraband or smuggled material."

"Oh Mr. Manesty, you are a true friend," John exclaimed. "That would be a great experience for me, and we surely need the funds."

Smuggling was very common in those days. Ships' captains would make only a partial listing of their cargo, thus paying a smaller duty on tobacco, rum, coffee, and the like and in this way make a bigger profit. John's job would be to board incoming vessels and check them. He also would keep close watch on docks and arrange for fast boats to patrol the coast. It was a big responsibility.

With mingled emotions, John broke the news to his wife. "Mary, darling, our good friend Mr. Manesty has gotten me a very good job, but I will have to move to Liverpool." He kept his eyes fixed on Mary's face, watching her reaction. But her wan face lit up. "That's wonderful, John. I'm so happy for you...Liverpool is a big city, isn't it?"

"Yes, it has a population of about 23,000...quite a contrast from the small towns we have been accustomed to. But Mary, you're in no condition to come with me; you could never stand life in a big city...."

"Now John, don't you worry one bit about me. I will be just fine. As soon as I recover, I will join you. Now you go and don't fret."

Gathering a few belongings, in August, 1755, John moved to Liverpool, rented a room and began to learn his new trade. During his first week he made a seizure. The goods were condemned and half of their value given to Newton. This of course made him happy. It was the nature of his work that he would be very busy at times and then would have leisure periods when he would just have to be in his office and delegate responsibilities to his men.

At first, Newton discovered that he had become overly concerned about money. This was because Mary's brother Jack, now a prosperous lawyer, kept urging John to buy a better home and make a place for Mary in genteel society.

Because of this pressure—even though when he took the job he had signed an oath that he would not take any fees other than his salary—he fell into the temptation of taking "unofficial gifts." But his conscience troubled him and after he talked to an evangelical minister about it, he stopped the practice. His income was considerably lessened, but he and his wife decided to live within their income. Mary was very gracious about it and agreed with the conscientious action her husband had taken.

One day when he was not particularly busy, he leaned back in his big office chair, praying and thinking. "God, I can't thank you enough for finding me this job. Thank you for the times of leisure when I can pray and study. Thank you that I am in a city with so many spiritual advantages, so many good evangelical meetings and friends. Lord, I could not have chosen a better situation. But..."

His face clouded...."But Lord, you know my deep fears and heartbreak over Mary. I'm torn between my joy in this new work, my evangelical friends, and my love for Mary—my constant torment that the next time I visit her will be my last."

After the difficulties of learning a new job were over and he settled into a routine, John discovered just how ideal his job was. He had the privacy of his own office as well as periods of leisure time. Without thinking twice, he knew what he would do with his time. Soon the bookcase was filled with his Bible, other versions for reference study, devotional books, volumes of poetry, good litera-ture, and the like.

When the physicians said they could do no more for Mary, John's grief was multiplied. But one day he con-fided to a friend, "How wonderful is the grace of God! The very day before I was to leave on my last visit, the Lord lifted the burden and gave me such great peace of mind, that I was able to leave her in the hands of the Lord in restful committal."

Strangely, not long after this committal of his dearest treasure, Mary began to amend. Within two months she was so completely recovered that she was able to join her husband in Liverpool. What a wonderful surprise and gift from God! And how grateful they were for His mercies. In October they rented a comfortable house and life became smooth and normal again.

On weekends and on his evenings off John continued to attend evangelical meetings. The evangelical or Methodist movement had begun in England in about 1738 and by 1755 was quite well established and widespread. Those who attended were derisively nicknamed the Dissenters.

(John vaguely remembered that his mother had begun attending the meetings in the early days.) John and his wife continued attending services of the State Church of which they were officially members, but he preferred the freedom and more scriptural teachings of the evangelicals.

It was a great event when the famous George Whitefield came to Liverpool for meetings. The tabernacle which held 5,000 was often so crowded that hundreds were turned away. To accommodate the working people, Whitefield held services at four o'clock in the morning. With great excitment, John joined the crowd who came. Because it was still dark, many carried lanterns, keeping their lights on until daylight. Later Newton said, "It was like a foretaste of heaven." He revelled in the joyful gospel songs (sometimes as many as twenty were interspersed in the three-hour-long meeting). He loved the atmosphere of joy and praise and the presence of God, climaxed by an enthusiastic scriptural sermon. It was all so unlike the staid worship of the formal State Church.

In his newly found spiritual joy, John was somewhat troubled about his wife's reaction, yet felt he should not pressure her into his way of believing. But to his great delight, his wife one day said to him, "John, I am a little hurt. You go to these evangelical meetings so often but never ask me to accompany you."

John caught her in his arms in a loving embrace. "Why Mary, dear...these are Dissenters, everywhere spoken against. You belong to the Established Church...I just didn't think you would be interested...I didn't want to push..."

"Now John," she interrupted, "you never consulted me about all this....May I come along tonight?"

"Of course dear; oh I would be so happy to have you with me. But I warn you, these meetings are different...."

At first Mary just sat there taking everything in as an observer, making no critical comments. One day she said, "Yes, these people are different, the meetings are different; but I like them. I really do. There is such a presence of God, such joy, such freedom in worship, such singing!"

John was overjoyed as he noticed that Mary took to the meetings like a duck to water and in not many months was almost as devoted to the Lord as he was. She was now a far cry from the social butterfly she had been in Chatham where she loved parties and went to church simply because it was fashionable.

But though his wife approved, many of John's friends did not. Even his dear friend Joseph Manesty warned,

"John, I'm afraid you are hurting your good reputation by associating with these people. It seems most of them are of the lower class. Genteel society wouldn't think of mingling with such."

"But Mr. Manesty," replied John, "doesn't the gospel include everybody? If Jesus associated with what you call the lower classes, is it wrong if I do?"

Not only did many of Newton's friends disapprove, but also his wife's relatives. Mrs. Catlett said to Mary, "I didn't think my daughter would ever stoop to mix so freely with washerwomen and chimney sweeps."

"Why mother," replied Mary, "I am surprised at you! I don't consider myself above these people; they may be of a different social class, but we are all brothers and sisters in the Lord."

"I grant you that," her mother replied. "But you also have brothers and sisters in the Church of England. Why can't you be content with that?"

"Their services are cold and formal. It's so refreshing and spiritually uplifting to attend these evangelical meetings. John and I still go to St. George's Cathedral, but we are fed spiritually by these despised Dissenters."

twenty-two

Growing in Grace

EANWHILE, DURING his leisure time John often sat before his big oak desk leaning over Bibles, books, pencil, and pad. Since he did not have a formal education, he studied Greek and Hebrew, read poetry and good books. Moreover, he discovered as he wrote his many letters that he had great facility in expressing himself in writing and even at times composed poems which he kept to himself. (Not realizing how this talent would later be used by the Lord.)

As he attended evangelical meetings and associated with their leaders, he had opportunities to give his personal testimony. It was the story of "a sinner saved by grace."

One thing which people observed in him was his fearlessness in associating with the Dissenters because they were denounced and even persecuted by the State Church.

High churchmen charged that the evangelicals encouraged "unhealthy emotionalism," and that when people of a weak and nervous temperament became obsessed with this doctrine, they "went mad." Bishops warned their people about becoming "tainted" by the meetings and demanded that they give up their "evangelical leanings." They made disparaging remarks that the meetings were attended only by the lower social classes, the poor and the ignorant.

It was true that the meetings did attract chiefly the common people, but it was also true that some nobility as well as members of the upper classes attended. Besides these, many university students came at the risk of being expelled from state-sponsored church colleges and seminaries.

Despite persecution and ridicule, the evangelical movement flourished and their churches became firmly established as an important minority in England. John steadfastly refused to be intimidated by the hierarchy of the church or by his relatives and even his close friends. The same independent spirit which in his early youth made him rebel against rules and regulations now gave him the courage to stand up for his personal convictions.

But to offend his good friend and benefactor did cost him a heartache, for when Joseph Manesty invited John and Mary to accompany him to Drury Lane Theatre to see a play, Newton had to use great diplomacy yet firmness when he declined the invitation.

This action disturbed even his loyal wife, for she said, "Mr. Manesty has shown you many favors. I think we should exercise a little prudence. Also, I think we ought to associate more with some of the well-bred Methodists, in order to show people that all Dissenters are not so..."

"Are not so—what—my dear," John broke in. "If we are to be consistent, then we must decide once and for all, either to go along with the worldly members of the Established Church; or else take up our cross and follow Jesus. Really, Mary, I am more afraid of being considered cowardly than imprudent."

In time Mary fully agreed and when her sisters planned a visit to their little house on Edmond Street, Mary warned, "Our home is a place where God is worshipped and we permit nothing which would not glorify Him."

Every decision John made to follow Jesus wholly promoted his spiritual growth. He began holding services in his home where he witnessed to his guests and gave short talks.

As Newton continued his activities for the Lord and as he became more at ease in speaking in public, his friends began to comment, "Mr. Newton, you have the makings of a parson. Why don't you consider it?" But John always protested, "How can a man with such a sinful background presume to enter the sacred office of the ministry?"

Those feelings of unworthiness persisted until one day he read in Galatians 1:23 that the Apostle Paul preached the faith he once destroyed. John thought to himself, *Not that I am remotely like the apostle, but in this one thing I can claim similarity—that I once blasphemed God and destroyed the faith of many.*

On his 33rd birthday, he said to Mary, "I am going to spend the day fasting and praying concerning the Lord's will about the ministry." He went into his room early in the morning and did not emerge until five in the afternoon. As he came out of his "closet of prayer," his face aglow with the presence of God, Mary looked at him expectantly. "What have you decided, dear?"

Solemnly but joyfully he replied, "I believe, Mary, that the Lord wants me to enter the ministry to glorify His name and to bless His people."

"I'm glad, very glad for your decision," she replied.

"I dimly recall," added John, "that my dear mother had planned and prayed that I become a minister; and now may her prayers be answered."

This decision brought varied reactions. As soon as Mary's ever-solicitous mother heard, she said to her daughter, "Mary, don't you encourage John in this notion. You will always be poor, and we wouldn't want that. We want you to be prosperous and happy. Now you encourage him to keep his customs job where he makes a fairly decent living for you."

Mary looked at her mother in surprise. "But mother, I am not concerned about being poor. It would be a great honor to be the wife of a parson. Of course I will be happy."

With the encouragement of his wife and a few friends, on December 16, 1758, Newton applied to the Archbishop of York for ordination. To his great disappointment, the clergyman said, "I am very sorry, Mr. Newton, but it is against the rules and canons of the church to ordain you. We require a university education and seminary training." Then the Archbishop paused and added, "Of course you know the church does not approve of association with Dissenters. We consider them to be overly emotional and doctrinally incorrect."

Crestfallen, John left the parsonage and told Mary the sad news. After the intital shock over the refusal, John continued praying, determined not to give up. Meanwhile, he was invited to speak in various churches.

Up until this time he had been preaching a negative doctrine, stressing hell as a punishment for sinners. One day he visited a woman in jail and tried to "frighten her into heaven," but the woman was unmoved. So Newton changed his method. The next time he visited her, he talked about God's love for sinners. To his delight, the woman was deeply touched. This incident greatly influenced his future ministry and he began to stress the love of God, which increased his popularity as a lay preacher.

He continued applying to various Archbishops and Bishops for ordination but was refused for the same reasons. Eventually the townspeople began gossiping: "Did you hear that no one will ordain John Newton?...He is a good speaker, but he does have a poor background. And then with no seminary training, and his associating with Dissenters—he should know it would get him in trouble with the Church."

His brother-in-law Jack expressed displeasure about his "religious fanaticism" and tried to dissuade him. Even his spiritual friend Captain Clunie warned, "John, I heard of a customs official who was discharged because he preached in a Methodist church. You could lose your job for the same reason." Also, his friend Joseph Manesty disapproved.

It was a trying time for the Newtons. He received advice from friend and foe. "Why don't you join the Dissenters? Why don't you take some of the positions offered you in other denominations? Why don't you stop associating with the Dissenters. Why don't you...."

But John would permit nothing to discourage him. It took six years before he finally became ordained. Meanwhile he continued working as Tide Surveyor (and was not fired as his friend intimated he might be), studying and writing, witnessing and speaking whenever he had the opportunity.

One day after hearing his testimony in a small group someone said, "John, this is a wonderful story and should be in print. Why don't you write the story of your conversion?"

This seemed a good idea so he wrote *An Authentic Narrative* in the form of fourteen letters addressed to a minister friend. These were published in 1764. Almost immediately, *The Authentic Narrative* became popular in England and the American colonies. The demand became so great that nine editions were printed and some foreign translations. Newton received much fan mail as well as an invitation in early 1764 from a Presbyterian church in Yorkshire to be their minister. He had just about decided to accept, when the Lord intervened.

Through his many speaking engagements and especially through his book, he attracted the attention and later the friendship of Lord Dartmouth, a devout noble-man who had "evangelical leanings." Impressed by Newton's qualifications Lord Dartmouth felt he should lend his prestige to John's quest for someone to ordain him.

Dr. Green, Bishop of Lincoln, finally agreed to perform the ordination ceremony. Following that, the nobleman used his influence to also get John the promise of a church in Olney, England, to replace the retiring curate.

When Mrs. Catlett heard of this, she frowned: "Why that little town consists mostly of factory workers. I had hoped my daughter would live in a more genteel neighborhood like Hampstead, for instance."

"But my dear lady," Newton reasoned, "doesn't the scripture say that the poor would have the gospel preached to them—that the common people heard Jesus gladly? I feel honored that the Lord should permit me to help the poor lacemakers of Olney." And Mary, who was always supportive, agreed.

But her family remained unhappy about this. Mr. Catlett wrote her daughter that a friend could get John the curacy at Hampstead. But Mary replied, "I doubt if he will change his mind." Mary's brother Jack was indignant. "But he will get twenty pounds a year more in Hampstead! He'd be a fool to turn down an opportunity like that!"

Even Newton's friend Captain Clunie urged John to consider Hampstead. "There are many fine people in that village," he wrote, "even some of distinction. In Olney you would be cut off from friends of your own social standing. Think about it, John; you owe it to your wife."

But neither Mary's family nor Captain Clunie understood the depth of the dedication of John and his wife, and they remained firm in their decision concerning Olney.

Before he could go, however, it was the rule of the church that he must first be ordained in St. George's church in Liverpool.

It was an important and eventful day for John and Mary. First, carriages began arriving. Then people came on foot from surrounding streets, the ladies attired in their Sunday best—ribbons and laces adorning billowing taffeta skirts; the gentlmen in fitted velvet waiscoats, ruffled shirts, knee breeches and brass buckles. Most of the men wore the white wigs then in fashion.

After all were settled in pews and the ladies had finished adjusting their skirts, all eyes were fixed at the front of the church. From a side door visiting preachers filed in and sat on ornate, high-backed chairs. Then John Newton walked in with appropriate measured tread, dressed in a borrowed gown and cassock. And finally, the most important guest of the day, Dr. Green, Bishop of Lincoln, resplendent in his robes.

As Newton sat rigidly, nervous about preaching his first sermon before such a distinguished audience, he glanced over the congregation. There amid the dignitaries was his friend Joseph Manesty. In the front pew sat Mary, hands gripping her Bible, eyes registering both concern and pride. *How handsome he looks, how dignified, how spiritual,* she thought.

The service proceeded at a leisurely pace. The organ solemnly peeled Bach's chorale; the choir anthemed the praises of Almighty God. The deacon droned announcements. Finally, Newton stepped into the pulpit. (How fervently Mary prayed, "Lord help him do well.")

In that day it was expected that Anglican ministers would deliver a two-hour written sermon. Although Newton had preached extemporaneously in the fervent style of the evangelicals, he now followed the Anglican custom. Because he was near-sighted he read his sermon with his head down, hardly lifting his eyes from his papers. At the same time he attempted to include in his delivery a little of the evangelical fervor.

As time dragged on, Mary winced. "Oh dear, I don't think he is making much of a first impression. I have heard him do much better in evangelical churches. He is trying to be two kinds of people, and it just isn't working."

At the conclusion of the service, people politely praised the new parson, but John considered himself a total failure.

Since part of the ordination procedure was that he was required to preach several sermons at St. George's, he determined to profit by his mistakes.

The next time, he tried the extemporaneous method, not using notes and trusting the Lord to supply the ideas. But after the service his wife overheard some ladies complain, "Gracious, but Rev. Newton is too loud and excitable...And he didn't keep to his subject." When Mary told her husband he said, "Will you give me your honest opinion? I want to do my very best during this trial period. Tell me, is it true that I was too loud and too long and didn't keep to my subject?"

Mary hesitated. "You did better this time, but yes, your sermon could be shorter; and yes, without notes you tend to wander. And yes, to people not accustomed to Dissenters' meetings, you might seem overly enthusiastic."

John embraced his wife. "You are right, my dear, very right. Now by the help of the Lord, things will change. I will shorten my sermons. And as for being loud and enthusuastic, by God's help I will observe neither Anglican ways nor Evangelical ways, but will try to follow the leading of the Lord, as well as common sense."

From that time, John did so much better that he had far greater acceptance than he expected. And when he finally left for Olney many people of all ranks were genuinely sorry to see him go.

twenty-three

Life in Olney
1764 - 1779

ND SO in 1764 when John was thirty-nine and Mary thirty-five, they moved to Olney.

As Newton became acquainted with his congregation, he learned that the forme pastor had favored the evangelical message and had led a number to the Lord. This encouraged Newton to incorporate some of his personal convictions into his ministry. True, he was an Anglican preacher, but definitely "with evangelical leanings."

First, he decided that one-hour sermons were long enough. For he said, "When weariness begins, edification ends...I would rather feed my people like chickens—a little at a time and more often—than stuff them like turkeys being fattened for slaughter."

He had not patience with theological disputes and was very tolorant of the views of other denominations, saying, "If I thought a person feared sin, loved the Word of God and was seeking Jesus, I would not walk the length of my study to proselyte him to the Calvinist doctrine."

Rather than doctrine he emphasized the abundant life and the joy of a close walk with God. Though he decried sin, he never ceased to proclaim the love of God (always remembering the mercy shown him in his former sinful state).

He later began the custom of inviting to his house for dinner all who had walked six or more miles to come to church. This involved great expense as well as work for Mary. But John insisted, "The Lord will provide." And He did.

The wealthy merchant John Thornton (who was introduced to him by Lord Dartmouth) wrote John: "Be hospitable; keep an open house for such as are worthy, help the poor and needy. I will allow the necessary funds and will send you more when you request it."

Small wonder that the church began filling with as many as 2,000 villagers eager to hear him. Not only were his good deeds an attraction but his delivery continually improved until he became an excellent preacher.

As word got around concerning his success, he received invitations to speak in other churches. Sometimes he preached twelve sermons in one week. He also continued receiving letters from all over England and overseas concerning his book *An Authentic Narrative.*

And so the uneducated, former great sinner who was refused ordination by six high churchmen became quite famous!

One day Lord Dartmouth, who closely followed

his protégé's progress, said, "My dear friend, I am proud of your success. You have fully vindicated my confidence in your ability. Little Olney was a good place to begin, but now that you are experienced and popular, I am offering you a position as president of a college in Savannah, Georgia. You will be working in a much larger city with a better salary."

John was so delighted he was tempted to accept at once but said, "I appreciate your confidence and am flattered, Lord Dartmouth. But I will have to pray about this matter. Do you mind waiting for my answer?"

"Not at all," replied the nobleman, "I respect your desire to seek God's will; that is one of the reasons for your success."

After prayer, Newton felt it was not the Lord's will, so he continued his work in Olney with renewed vigor. Despite his mother-in-law's complaint about his "excessive familiarity with the poor," Newton took time to visit their humble cottages.

Whenever Mary accompanied him, he noticed that she paid special attention to children. One day as they walked home John said, "Mary, apparently we are not going to have children. I know you feel sad about this; I can tell by the longing way you gaze at the children in these homes."

Mary sighed. "Yes, John, year after year I had hoped that God would give us children; I know you are also disappointed."

They walked on in silence, each feeling the other's

sadness, until John said, "Perhaps the Lord is withholding children from us so that we can love the children of our parishioners."

So John filled this vacancy by playing with children, telling them stories, giving them sweets. And in a day when the spiritual needs of children were not understood, he was innovative and courageous enough to hold classes for them. He taught the fear and love of God, hymns and scriptures, just as he remembered his mother doing for him. At one time as many as 200 children attended his classes.

In 1767, a widow named Mrs. Unwin and the poet William Cowper moved to Olney, mainly in order to benefit from the spiritual help they received from Newton. Since there was no intellectual fellowship among the ignorant classes in Olney, John and Mary were delighted with the company of these two.

When John discovered that the poet also loved nature, the two often walked together long distances to places where John was to speak. The ladies also had good times—Mary delighting in showing her new friend her garden and sharing recipes with her. In the evening the four often met at the parsonage for fellowship, which usually included sitting around the harpsichord singing hymns and ending with prayer.

One day Newton confided to Cowper, "I suppose you are aware that as an Anglican minister I am obliged to confine myself largely to their tenets and methods. But I am convinced that among my parishioners are those who desire more intimacy with God. I wish I knew how to help these hungry-hearted ones."

As they conversed, Newton cried, "I've got it, why not hold cottage meetings? There I would be at liberty to fully preach the gospel."

And so it was announced at the next service: "We will be holding informal cottage meetings every Tuesday night. All are welcome." The meetings became a blessing to many, but both Newton and the poet Cowper soon realized that the solemn hymns used in the Anglican church services were not suitable for cottage meetings.

Newton had already been writing poetry, but never for the public. Now, with the encouragement of Cowper, he wrote poems about his personal experiences with God. They were set to music and eventually compiled into *The Olney Hymnal.* Sixty-eight of the songs were written by Cowper and 280 by Newton.

In one of Newton's songs—"In Evil Long I Took Delight"—he depicts the experiences of a sinner who met God.

Another song—"How Sweet The Name of Jesus Sounds"—shows the close fellowship Newton had with God.

> *How sweet the name of Jesus sounds*
> *In a believer's ear;*
> *It soothes his sorrows, heals his wounds*
> *And drives away his fear.*
> *Dear name! The rock on which I build,*
> *My shield and hiding place;*
> *My never-failing treasury,*
> *Filled with boundless stores of grace.*

Despite his great love of nature, nothing took the place of his love of God. He expressed this in "How Tedious, How Tasteless":

> *How tedious and tasteless*
> *The hours when Jesus no longer I see;*
> *Sweet prospects, sweet birds and sweet flowers*
> *Have all lost their sweetness to me;*
> *The midsummer sun shines but dim*
> *The fields strive in vain to look gay.*
> *But when I am happy in Him*
> *December's as pleasant as May.*

Thornton bought and distributed the first thousand copies of *The Olney Hymnal* After that thousands more were sold in England and the colonies. Some of the best of these hymns can still be found in hymnals, the most familiar being of course "Amazing Grace."

Because of his growing fame Newton was constantly tempted to pride. Often he would sit back in his office chair and deliberately muse over the scripture which he had placed on the wall facing him:

Since thou was precious in my sight, thou hast been honorable. But that thou shouldst remember that thou wast a bondman in the land of Egypt and the Lord thy God redeemed thee....(Deut. 15:15)

And he would pray earnestly, "Lord help me, keep me humble."

One day he said to his wife, "All I need to do to keep down pride is to mix a little Plantane sauce with my savory diet," (in remembrance of his humiliations on the Plantane Islands).

He constantly reminded himself that he had been an infidel, a blasphemer and a great sinner. That he was self-educated; that it was only through the kindness of Lord Dartmouth that he had been ordained and given a pastorate. "I am nothing, Lord," he prayed, "nothing. You are all. It is all of grace."

Of course he realized that his pastorate was in a small and poor town. Nevertheless he showed himself to be true to God and to his ministry and did not long for a curacy in a "more genteel neighborhood."

Despite his many duties, he took time to maintain some contact with his stepmother. He learned that for many years she had ridiculed his evangelical beliefs; but after her children were grown, she became a devout Christian. His half-brother William, a debauched infidel, died at thirty years. His half-sister was happily married. And his other half-brother Harry now served with the Royal Navy in Boston, due to the influence of Thornton.

After ten years in Olney, Newton was nearly fifty and middle-aged. He slowed his pace somewhat and accepted fewer invitations to speak.

One day as he was trying on a suit he had not worn for a while he noticed that it had become much too small. "Mary," he said, "Just look at me. I'm getting too stout. I will have to try harder to be more moderate in eating."

Mary, who was in the kitchen baking cookies, replied,

"I'll help by not baking so often."

"Oh dear," John replied, "why not begin next week." And they both laughed merrily.

However, it was not easy to be moderate, for it was an age of gluttony in which the more affluent literally stuffed themselves far beyond the needs of their bodies.

Moreover, during his pastoral visits he was always served tea and dessert. So between his efforts not to offend his hostess and his determination not to overeat, and his own enjoyment of sweets, he had a constant battle.

Another problem—which he did not expect to have—was that at times his mind would flood with all kinds of evil thoughts, memories of his wicked and sinful days in the past. But as he struggled against them in prayer, he always gained the power to overcome and to set his mind on things above.

A constant source of distress also was what John called his idolatrous love of Mary. During their 11th year in Olney they celebrated their 25th anniversary.

"Mary," he said, "I love you more now than when I first met you. The Lord holds first place in my heart, but I must admit, you are a close second. I'm afraid I'm making an idol of you. Oh Mary, what would I do without you! I love you too much!"

"Please don't condemn yourself," Mary often replied; "I am sure that I am not your idol. You constantly prove your love for God and His people."

"No, Mary, you are *the one*. After conducting a service, you don't know how glad I am to return to the warmth and brightness of you in the home."

And so he continued to delight in the woman who had won his heart when he was just a youth of seventeen years and whom he had never forgotten during his years of affliction at sea and on the Plantane Islands. After his conversion, his love took on another quality, being now mingled with the love of God. And when they settled in Olney with its countryside and woods, his happiness was full.

It was a busy and happy time for him preaching and publishing letters and articles of spiritual depth. He became known as a religious writer of note.

Time moved on. During their fifteenth year at Olney Newton noticed that church attendance began to decline and wondered if his parishioners were getting rather tired of him. Some continued to complain that he was too familiar with the poor, others that he was too narrow and intolerant of what he called "worldly pleasures" and that in stressing love, he was too lenient toward sinners.

Whatever the cause or combination of causes, he felt it was time for a change, both for the congregation at Olney and for himself and Mary.

twenty-four

St. Mary's of Woolnoth
London, 1779

SINCE JOHN Newton was now fifty-four (in those days it was considered a rather mature age) he became anxious about his future. But as he and Mary prayed, they became confident that the Lord had a plan and would provide.

It was his friend John Thornton whom the Lord used.

"My good man," he said one day, "you have done very well at Olney and are loved and known all over England. Now I have a proposition for you. Several congregations have combined with St. Mary's of Woolnoth in London and are looking for a pastor. Would you consider it?"

Totally surprised, Newton replied, "Oh thank you very much, Mr. Thornton, but I am not qualified to pastor such an important church."

But Mr. Thornton would not hear of it. "You most certainly are! You are famous and will attract many to the services. People need what you can give them. And by the way, it is one of the few large churches which is dominated by the evangelicals."

Newton immediately perked up. "Oh, is that so? That is indeed interesting. Perhaps you are right. Will you give me time to pray about this?"

"Of course, my dear friend, but don't take too long." The two men shook hands and parted.

That evening at supper John said, "Mary, what would you think of my pastoring St. Mary's of Woolnoth in London?" His eyes twinkled. Mary held her fork in mid-air. "Now John, what kind of far-fetched tale is that? It's not like you to be building such fine castles in the air." And she proceeded with her meal.

"London," John mused, "that great metropolis, the capital of England."

"Cities!" his wife frowned. "We had a taste of city life in Liverpool and I must say I prefer the quietness of little Olney. How happily these fifteen years have passed!"

"Yes, I agree. The countryside, the woods, how we love that. But now we may be leaving Olney for something entirely different." And he told her of the offer of Mr. Thornton.

At first Mary was stunned. "My, what a great honor."

Then she was silent a moment and said, "But strangely, I'm not thinking of that." Almost with one consent they both left the table and walked to the window where they could see Mary's garden, lush with vegetables and flowers. Beyond lay fields and streams, trees and woods. All those places where he and his friend Cowper had walked and enjoyed nature and talked of the kingdom of God.

Places where he and Mary had wandered, hand in hand, stopping to listen to the song of the thrush or to admire a clump of wild daisies. This was their element.

"Mary," said John as he pointed outside, "are you willing to exchange tall trees for tall buildings, the song of birds for the sounds of commerce; quietness for the publicity that accompany fame and honor?"

As he and Mary looked into each other's eyes, Mary said, "John, you have always placed God's will above your preferences."

"I know. I know. I have been praying...and I believe this is God's will."

That evening before they retired, Newton wrote Thornton a letter of acceptance.

Not long afterwards John went to London to look for a house. During his prayerful search John was delighted to find a comfortable home in Charles Square. As he examined the rooms, he looked out of the kitchen window and gasped in surprise.

Beyond the backyard lay a small field with cows grazing. "Cows, a field, birds," he exclaimed with delight. "How good of God to lead me here."

He could hardly wait to return to Olney to tell Mary the joyful news. It took only a few days to pack their personal belongings (the furniture would remain in the Olney parsonage).

Then began the farewells, first to the poet Cowper and Mrs. Unwin; then to their congregation. Finally, the long ride to London in the jolting carriage, each occupied with wondering about the future.

When they finally arrived, John first showed her the house—a typical middle class structure with high ceilings and dark walnut woodwork, furnished with some pieces of old but elegant furniture. Then John took her into the kitchen to show her the view. "Oh John," she cried, "fields, wild flowers. And look, see that meadow lark. He is singing to welcome us." And they hugged each other with delight.

St. Mary's of Woolnoth church was situated in the heart of London and had a membership of shopkeepers, artisans, and rich merchants. Therefore, preaching his first sermon at St. Mary's was quite different than at Olney. Because Newton had become so popular as a preacher, author and hymn writer, such crowds of visitors from surrounding areas came to hear him that regular members complained they could not always find room in their own pews.

When Newton learned that his congregation had varied theological beliefs, he wisely said little about doctrines. Instead he emphasized the evangelical message of a personal relationship with Jesus and loving growth in Him. And the hungry-hearted received the Word eagerly.

By this time the evangelicals, through the preaching of Wesley, Whitefield and others had formed their own denominations, the main one being Methodist. And although Newton was aware of the contempt with which these Dissenters were still held (particularly by the nobility, the aristocratic upper classes and the theologians), he continued attending their meetings and associating with their people.

Not long after he took his new pastorate, people began coming to his home for counsel and spiritual help. Eventually this grew into his popular breakfast parties, attended by ministers of the state church, Dissenters, prominent laymen and university and seminary students.

They came for different reasons. Most came for spiritual help, but some out of curiosity, to get a closer look at this man who was once such a sinner.

In one of his many letters to friends he wrote, "I live a strange life of busy idleness...My time is divided between running about to look after people and sitting at home like a tame elephant or monkey, waiting for people to look at me."

One of those who came "to look at him" was Sir Charles Middleton, comptroller of the Royal Navy and member of Parliament. Oddly, Sir Charles in his youth had been a midshipman at the time when Newton was also on the HMS *Harwich.*

None of these honors moved Newton. When a New Jersey university offered him an honorary degree of Doctor of Divinity he declined, saying, "The dreary coast of Africa was the university to which the Lord was pleased to send me, and I dare not acknowledge a relation to any other."

He would never allow himself to forget the pit from which he had been dug and loved to sing his own composition:

> *Amazing grace, how sweet the sound,*
> *That saved a wretch like me.*
> *I once was lost but now am found,*
> *Was blind, but now I see.*

In his own eyes he was still only a sinner saved by God's great mercy.

The story of his conversion—*An Authentic Narrative*—continued to be widely read. He also wrote two other books, *Omicron* and *Cardiphonia*, a collection of spiritual letters.

Although he remained a minister of the State Church many of his views were unorthodox. During a breakfast party a pastor asked if infants who died before being baptized were saved. Newton replied, "I believe they are saved, baptized or not. I cannot think that the salvation of a soul depends on a negligent curate who cannot be found to baptize a dying infant." He also had his own views regarding the Sabbath. One day he was notified that the Lord Mayor would visit St. Mary's to hear a sermon in aid of a charity school. It was customary after such services to attend a ceremonial dinner at the Manor House. Although few clergymen saw anything wrong with having this event on a Sunday, Newton did not approve.

For over a week he tried to find an excuse to stay away without insulting the Lord Mayor. Then God rescued Newton by allowing him to trip in his own home and dislocate his shoulder. With arm in sling, he was readily excused! Privately Newton smiled at the tactics the Lord used to rescue him.

He was honest and outspoken. When an overly zealous deacon suggested a prayer circle on Sunday evenings, Newton replied, "That may be a good idea. But after preaching in the morning and late afternoon, by the time nine o'clock comes, I am more disposed for supper and bed than for prayers."

Speaking of suppers, in London he had a still greater struggle against overeating, since he was so often invited out. In a letter he described a menu at Manor House: "Fowl, game, beef, lamb, pudding, pastry, confectionary, fruit, ice and burgundy." It took much will power to restrain himself in the presence of others who ate so heartily.

But he complained to his wife more than once, "Mary, I don't like to overeat. First, because I don't want to be a glutton and second, when my stomach is too full, my head is empty, and I cannot think clearly."

Not only was he an independent thinker regarding some of the practices of the Anglican church, but he was beginning to have different ideas about the slave trade. The English rationalized that Negroes were happier as slaves of enlightened Englishmen. And that since as heathen they would go to hell, as slaves they might be converted to Christianity.

But Newton could never forget the pitiful sight of slaves in chains, slaves dying and being dumped into the ocean like animals. He had secretly been hoping that the slave trade would some day be abolished. And now it seemed the day was coming.

About this time Newton received a letter requesting a conference, to be kept secret because the writer William Wilberforce, who at that time was 26 years old and already distinguished, was a member of Parliament. (Later he became very famous in the English government.) As a result of the initial visit—even though Newton was 34 years older than the young seeker after God—a close bond was formed between the two. After that they had frequent (though secret) conferences, in which Newton was a spiritual guide to Wilberforce.

In 1780, some courageous people—mainly Dissenters and poets—began to decry slavery. Later Wilberforce joined them and in 1787 became one of the early leaders of an organization which worked to abolish slavery.

Newton considered himself too old then to actively engage in campaigning, but supported Wilberforce by writing articles which greatly influenced public opinion against the slave trade. One of the most well known was a long pamphlet *Thoughts Upon The African Slave Trade*. Thousands were printed and distributed throughout England. His articles were especially convincing because of his experiences as captain of slave ships.

Because of the strenuous efforts of Wilberforce and others, slavery was abolished in England in 1804. Newton wrote to Wilberforce, congratulating him and expressing his thankfulness for the great moral victory won for his nation. (It was not until after the Civil War that America made the same decision.)

twenty-five

The Last Years

A S TIME passed John remained deeply devoted to his Mary. Even when he was away for a few days, he wrote her and addressed his letters to "My dear, sweet, precious one." Mary's frail health was a constant heartache to him. She never was really sick or really well. In October, 1788, when her husband was on a speaking engagement, she secretly went to a famous surgeon.

As he examined her he pressed a sore place on her left breast. "Did you ever injure yourself here?"

"Yes, long ago. I fell and hurt myself there."

"And you have been feeling increasing tenderness?"

"Yes, Doctor. In fact, it has really begun to pain me."

The doctor was silent a while. "My dear lady, I am very sorry, but you have an advanced cancer. There is nothing I can do."

Mary stared at him. "Doctor...I can't believe it. Can't you remove this...thing...can't you...?"

"I'm sorry, Mrs. Newton, but by the time a cancer has progressed this far, it is too late for surgery. If I had known this long ago..."

White-faced and trembling, Mary asked, "How much time do I have?"

"A year, a year and a half at the most." Lifting her head, Mary said, "Then I will live that time to the fullest, by God's grace."

When her husband returned from his trip, he knew that something was terribly wrong. At first Mary tried to make light of it, but finally told him. Soberly, John looked into his wife's face, so stricken he could hardly speak. "Mary, I can't believe this. We were so happy. I thought we would have many more years together. How can this be?" He clasped her tightly to his heart and they both wept.

"God is punishing me because I idolize you too much," John sobbed.

"No John, don't say that. God is not like that. And I insist you have not made an idol of me. You love God with all your heart. Let us just accept this as God's will."

That night John could not sleep. "God's will, God's will," he kept thinking. "God, help me not to rebel. Help me, help me."

As he mechanically went about his duties the next day, his heart leaden, it seemed to him that it couldn't be true; and yet it was. He knew he should submit to God's will, just as he himself had so often preached. But he confessed to a friend, "I am more likely to toss like a bull in a net than to be reconciled." But as he continued to pray, God did quiet his heart and help him accept this great sorrow.

As her illness progressed, Mary gradually retired from public life, then from household duties and finally was confined to bed. How John's heart ached as he watched her become more frail and wasted!

For nearly a year Mary lay in bed, cheerful and patient, reading her Bible, singing hymns. After services, Newton hurried to her room and during the last few weeks left her bedside only to preach. She died quietly on December 15, 1790, at the age of sixty-one. They had been married forty wonderful years.

Even though he knew his Mary would not live, when he finally lost her, John was crushed. As he wandered about the house he said, "Her image follows me in every room." Despite his grief, he refused to permit himself to retreat from life. The very next day after the funeral he went for his usual walk, greeting people, and chatting with them.

He continued preaching and overseeing the breakfas meetings and tried to keep to his old routines. Years before, as he had pondered the possibility of her death, he had determined that his life would thereafter be governed by Habakkuk 3:18: "Yet I will rejoice in the Lord; I will joy in the God of my salvation." As he determined to do so, the same grace that brought him salvation also brought him comfort and peace.

But it was five years before he could say, "The wound is healed. I no longer have acute sorrow. My beloved is with the Lord and happy in Him. I will be glad in the Lord."

He never remarried but remained in the parsonage, having housekeepers and later his niece Betsy care for him. During the next seventeen years without Mary, he continued to preach at St. Mary's of Woolnoth and in other churches, as guest speaker and continued his writing ministry.

As he approached his 80th year his memory began to fail and his preaching became less effective. He commented humorously to a friend, "I never knew before what it was to be seventy-nine." Even so, people came to hear the grand old man because of what he was and had been.

Yet age continued its toll. Although his health was good and he was cheerful, his memory, hearing, and vision steadily failed.

The inevitable day arrived. In October, 1806, as he started to preach, he completely forgot what he was about to say. A deacon had to go into the pulpit to refresh his memory. At first when someone had suggested retirement, he had shouted in a quavering voice, "What, shall the former blasphemer stop telling of the glory of God while I can still speak!" But now he finally admitted, "Yes, I can see it is time to retire."

During October, 1806, he entered the pulpit for the last time. The occasion was to raise money for the sufferers from the battle of Trafalgar. It was appropriate, for Newton had once served in the navy. The event brought back many memories:

The time when he was forcibly recruited on the navy ship the HMS *Harwich*; the bitter days as the wicked and blasphemous sailor on slave ships; the hardships and humiliations while working for Claw on the Plantane Islands. And how after the storm at sea he had experienced the wonderful grace of God in his salvation, which he had been preaching now for over forty years. What memories!

After his retirement he declined drastically. As he realized death was near he said, "I am like a person going on a journey in a stagecoach, who expects its arrival hourly and often gets up and looks out of the window for it."

Near the close of his life he told a friend at his bedside, "My memory is nearly gone, but I can still remember two things: That I am a great sinner and that Christ is a great Savior."

He died in 1807 at the age of eighty-two.

The former blasphemer who preached the faith he had once destroyed entered the heaven he once said did not exist. Who knows but that he is now singing the last verse of his song "Amazing Grace":

> *"When we've been there ten thousand years,*
> *Bright shining as the sun,*
> *We've no less days to sing His praise*
> *Than when we first begun."*

postscript

Before his death, Newton wrote a letter for the direction of his executors:

"I propose writing an epitaph for myself, if it may be put on a plain marble tablet near the vestry door, to the following purport:

> John Newton, Clerk
> Born 1725 Died (1807)
> Once an infidel and libertine
> A servant of slaves in Africa
> Was, by the rich mercy of our Lord and Savior
> *Jesus Christ*
> Preserved, restored, pardoned
> And appointed to preach the faith he had long labored to destroy.
> Near sixteen years at Olney in Bucks and (twenty-seven) years in St. Mary's of Woolnoth.
> On February 1, 1750, he married
> *Mary.*
> Daughter of the late George Catlett of Chatham, Kent. He resigned her to the Lord who gave her on the 15th day of December, 1790.

And I earnestly desire that no other monument and no inscription but to this purport may be attempted for me."

resource materials

Erwin, Grace, *Servant of Slaves.* Canada: William B. Eerdmans Publishing Co., 1961. Autobiography.

Heinemann, Bernard Martin William, *John Newton.* Ltd. 15-16 Queen Street Mayfair, London WIX 8 BE. Out of print.

Newton, John, *Letters of a Slave Trader Freed by God's Grace.* Chicago: Moody Press. Autobiography.

HEROES OF THE FAITH

This exciting biographical series explores the lives of famous Christian men and women throughout the ages. These trade paper books will inspire and encourage you to follow the example of these "Heroes of the Faith" who made Christ the center of their existence. 208 pages each. Only $3.97 each!

Gladys Aylward, Missionary to China
Sam Wellman

Brother Andrew, God's Undercover Agent
Alan Millwright

Corrie ten Boom, Heroine of Haarlem
Sam Wellman

William and Catherine Booth,
Founders of the Salvation Army
Helen Hosier

John Bunyan,
Author of The Pilgrim's Progress
Sam Wellman

William Carey, Father of Missions
Sam Wellman

Amy Carmichael, Abandoned to God
Sam Wellman

Fanny Crosby, the Hymn Writer
Bernard Ruffin

Frederick Douglass, Abolitionist and Reformer
Rachael Phillips

Jonathan Edwards, the Great Awakener
Helen Hosier

Jim Elliot, Missionary to Ecuador
Susan Miller

Charles Finney, the Great Revivalist
Bonnie Harvey

Billy Graham, the Great Evangelist
Sam Wellman

C. S. Lewis, Author of Mere Christianity
Sam Wellman

Martin Luther, the Great Reformer
Dan Harmon

George Müller, Man of Faith
Bonnie Harvey

Eric Liddell, Olympian and Missionary
Ellen Caughey

David Livingstone, Missionary and Explorer
Sam Wellman

George Washington Carver,
Inventor and Naturalist
Sam Wellman

D. L. Moody, the American Evangelist
Bonnie Harvey

Samuel Morris, the Apostle of Simple Faith
W. Terry Whalin

Mother Teresa, Missionary of Charity
Sam Wellman

Watchman Nee, Man of Suffering
Bob Laurent

John Newton, Author of "Amazing Grace"
Anne Sandberg

Florence Nightingale, Lady with the Lamp
Sam Wellman

Luis Palau, Evangelist to the World
Ellen Bascuti

Francis and Edith Schaeffer,
Defenders of the Faith
Sam Wellman

Mary Slessor, Queen of Calabar
Sam Wellman

Charles Spurgeon, the Great Orator
Dan Harmon

Hudson Taylor, Founder, China Inland Mission
Vance Christie

Sojourner Truth, American Abolitionist
W. Terry Whalin

William Tyndale, Bible Translator and Martyr
Bruce and Becky Durost Fish

John Wesley, the Great Methodist
Sam Wellman

George Whitefield, Pioneering Evangelist
Bruce and Becky Durost Fish

Available wherever books are sold.
Or order from:
Barbour Publishing, Inc.
P.O. Box 719
Uhrichsville, Ohio 44683
http://www.barbourbooks.com

If you order by mail, add $2.00 to your order for shipping.
Prices subject to change without notice.